Basics of Environmental Resource Management

Basics of Environmental Resource Management

Dr. Kamalesh Kumar

B Tech., MS, PhD

Assistant Professor

Birla Institute of Technology & Science (BITS)

Pilani, Rajasthan

Publishing Globally

NEW AGE INTERNATIONAL (P) LIMITED, PUBLISHERS

New Delhi • Bangalore • Chennai • Cochin • Guwahati

Hyderabad • Kolkata • Lucknow • Mumbai

Visit us at www.newagepublishers.com

Published by New Age International (P) Ltd., Publishers
First Edition: 2015

BRANCHES

- **Bangalore** 37/10, 8th Cross (Near Hanuman Temple), Azad Nagar, Chamarajpet Bangalore-560 018, Tel.: (080) 26756823, Telefax: 26756820 **E-mail: bangalore@newagepublishers.com**
- **Chennai** 26, Damodaran Street, T. Nagar, Chennai-600 017, Tel.: (044) 24353401 Telefax: 24351463, **E-mail: chennai@newagepublishers.com**
- **Cochin** CC-39/1016, Carrier Station Road, Ernakulam South, Cochin-682 016 Tel.: (0484) 2377004, Telefax: 4051303 **E-mail: cochin@newagepublishers.com**
- **Guwahati** Hemsen Complex, Mohd. Shah Road, Paltan Bazar, Near Starline Hotel Guwahati-781 008, Tel.: (0361) 2513881, Telefax: 2543669 **E-mail: guwahati@newagepublishers.com**
- **Hyderabad** 105, 1st Floor, Madhiray Kaveri Tower, 3-2-19, Azam Jahi Road Nimboliadda, Hyderabad-500 027, Tel.: (040) 24652456 Telefax: 24652457, **E-mail: hyderabad@newagepublishers.com**
- **Kolkata** RDB Chambers (Formerly Lotus Cinema) 106A, 1st Floor S.N. Banerjee Road, Kolkata-700 014, Tel.: (033) 22273773 Telefax: 22275247, **E-mail: kolkata@newagepublishers.com**
- **Lucknow** 16-A, Jopling Road, Lucknow-226 001, Tel.: (0522) 2209578, 4045297 Telefax: 2204098, **E-mail: lucknow@newagepublishers.com**
- **Mumbai** 142C, Victor House, Ground Floor, N.M. Joshi Marg, Lower Parel Mumbai-400 013, Tel.: (022) 24927869, Telefax: 24915415 **E-mail: mumbai@newagepublishers.com**
- **New Delhi** 22, Golden House, Daryaganj, New Delhi-110 002 Tel.: (011) 23262368, 23262370, Telefax: 43551305 **E-mail: sales@newagepublishers.com**

ISBN: 978-81-224-3669-3

₹ 150.00

C-14-04-7541

Printed in India at Ajit Printing Press, New Delhi.
Typeset at In-house. Delhi.

PUBLISHING GLOBALLY
NEW AGE INTERNATIONAL (P) LIMITED, PUBLISHERS
7/30 A, Daryaganj, New Delhi - 110002
Visit us at **www.newagepublishers.com**

Dedicated to

Shri P.K. Shaha

My Late Father-in-Law

Preface

The main objective of this book ***'Basics of Environmental Resource Management'*** is to bring together and integrate in a single book the fundamental areas of environmental resource management. In chapter 1, concept of ecology has been presented in detail. Chapter 2 describes organizations involved in environmental resource management at International and National level. In chapter 3, fundamentals of environmental impact assessment has been presented. Basic details of environmental resource management and environmental audit has been given in chapters 4 and 5 respectively. Finally in chapter 6, state of natural resources in India and state of environmental pollution in India has been described in detail. Final year undergraduate and first year graduate students of civil engineering will find the subject matter of the book quite useful. General readers interested in knowing the fundamentals of environmental resource management will also find the contents of the book useful.

Review questions, given at the end of each chapter cover some of the key concepts of that chapter. However, students will be expected to be familiar with all the concepts given in each chapter. Since chapter 6 is on case studies, no review questions have been given at the end of this chapter.

Author is thankful to Mr. Rajendra K. Upadhye (former graduate student, civil engineering, Birla Institute of Technology & Science, Pilani), whose graduate project report (completed under author's supervision) was used as reference in chapters 2 and 6 of this book. Author is also thankful to Ms. Malvika Dixit (former undergraduate student, civil engineering, Birla Institute of Technology & Science, Pilani), whose undergraduate project report (completed under author's supervision) was used as reference in chapter 3 of this book.

Subject matter of the book can be covered in a course of one semester which is of about 4 to 4.5 months duration.

Suggestions to improve the usefulness of the book will be gratefully received.

KAMALESH KUMAR

Preface

Contents

1.1 INTRODUCTION

1

Ecology

1.1 INTRODUCTION

Ecology is the study of abundance and distribution of organisms. To study these things, ecologists must account for all influences on abundance and distribution. It has to be both in space and time. These influences include both abiotic (geography, climate, etc.) and biotic (other organisms from the same species, from other related species, from unrelated species).

Ecology is a science, but has important interactions with all areas of human endeavor. Ecology is the basis of **environmental science** (the study of man's effect on natural systems), **conservation biology** (the study of how to preserve natural systems undergoing human impact), **restoration ecology** (the study of means of restoring ecosystems altered by human activities to their pre-alteration state), and **environmental engineering** (the study of how we can manipulate the natural world to produce desired effects or to lessen the impact of disturbances caused by human activity).Ecologists interact with economists (to determine the costs of environmental change), with engineers (to predict and modify the effects of human activities), with sociologists and anthropologists (to understand how human society views, uses, and affects the natural environment), with ethicists and theologians (to understand about the basis of ethical behavior).

Ecology is a changing body of knowledge. As with all sciences, conclusions are reached on the basis of data analysis. Ecological data are often difficult and expensive to collect and interpret. Studies are often not conclusive or cannot be generalized. When a decision must be made on the basis of inconclusive data, it is often open to criticism. For example, locally, ecological data is needed to assess the impact of road building on those living in the Nashville area and to bring local and state agencies (and local businesses) into compliance with state and federal regulations concerning the environment.

Ecology is not something one can avoid even though one may attempt to ignore it. If you breath, eat, drink water (or beverages composed mostly of water), are affected by the weather, or are likely to get sick sometime in your life then you will depend on a natural system to supply a necessity. If you live on the Earth, then that natural system is being directly or indirectly affected by the human population. Direct affect by human population include, water supply, oxygen supply, food supply (oceanic fisheries, pollination, natural pest predators), extractive renewable commodities (wood, some fuels, some fertilizers), genes (increasingly important as our ability to manipulate genes increases) and recreation. Indirect affect by human population include, nutrient cycling, atmospheric regulation (CO_2, SO_2, O_3, NO_3 levels), climatic buffering (run-off control, heat dissipation, wind amelioration), waste elimination (sewage, agricultural pollution) and erosion control.

Ecology is organized into a hierarchical group of subdisciplines. **Behavioral ecology** is the study of how behavior of individuals affects their ability to survive and reproduce. Since, a population is composed of individuals, behavior directly impacts population level phenomena, such as population growth rate. **Autecology (or physiological ecology)** is the study of how physical factors; such as temperature change, seasonality, soil nutrient composition, affect the survival and reproduction of individual organisms. Notice that, in both of the definitions above, the focus is on what affects survival and reproduction, the core determinants of success or failure for individuals and populations. This focus is what makes these studies ecology and not behavioral science or physiology. **Population ecology** is the study of how groups of individuals (belonging to the same species) grow (or shrink) and exchange individuals with other populations nearby. Depending on the nature of the species, many factors may affect population growth (food availability or quality, predators, habitat change, etc.). **Community ecology** is the study of how populations from different species interact to mutually affect each other's population growth and survival. What composes a community is very changeable and depends on the organisms studied and the purposes of the investigator. The only commonality is that the different populations (representing different species) must interact with one another. Often, they will be similar species (e.g., the trees in a forest) as their similarity means they have similar habitat requirements and, most probably, will interact because of those needs. **Ecosystem ecology** is the study of how the flow of energy and matter takes place in large scale living systems. Ecosystem ecology is concerned with how nutrients enter, are recycled within, and leave the system; with what inputs of energy do the work in the system, how that energy is passed from one part of the system to another, and how energy leaves the system. Typically, the community studied in ecosystem ecology encompasses all organisms that are a part of the system. However, the emphasis is not on the organisms as much as it is on the flow of materials and energy between them.

In the process of converting radiant energy into chemical energy by photosynthesis, plants incorporate inorganic elements and compounds into its protoplasm. Carbon dioxide and water are important in this context, however nitrogen, phosphorous, sulfur and magnesium are also incorporated. As the green plants are grazed on, chemical energy in the form of carbohydrates, fats, proteins as well as host of nutrients are transferred to primary consumers. Further, they are transferred from primary consumers to secondary consumers and then to decomposers from all preceding levels. There is progressive diminuation of energy with transfer from one level to another, nutrient component is not diminshed. Some nutrients may even become concentrated in certain steps of transfer. Nutrient containing protoplasm is decomposed by decomposers and nutrients are released in environment. There they are available for reuse and recycling. A simplified model of energy and nutrient movement in ecosystem is shown in Fig. 1.1.

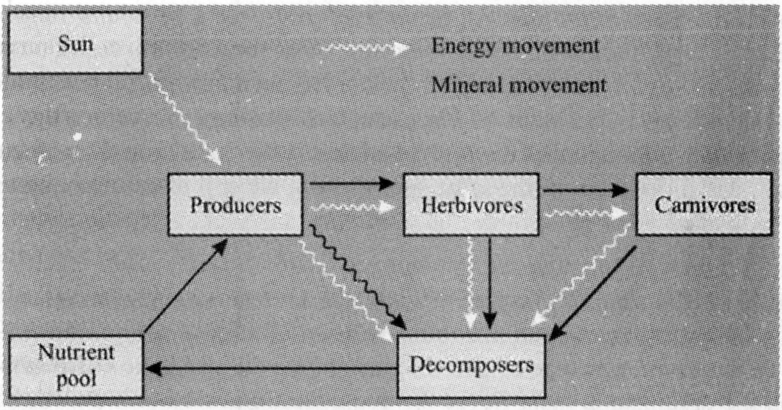

Fig. 1.1 Simplified model of energy and mineral movement in ecosystems

A good question to ask at this point is why organize the field of ecology in such a manner. Why not just study how individual animals react to different factors and add up these responses in some fashion to predict what to expect from nature? The answer lies in the concept of **emergent properties**. To understand this, we have to have a clear idea of what a hierarchy is. A hierarchy is a means of grouping units of something (individual animals, say) into nested levels of groups. Thus, in an organism, atoms are grouped into kinds of molecules, which are grouped into different kinds of organelles, which are grouped into different kinds of cells, which are grouped into different kinds of tissues, etc. This grouping is not just for convenience but is a real grouping (i.e. it exists in nature). The ecological hierarchy is real also, and we study it as such because some phenomena are only observable by studying a particular level of organization in the hierarchy. We study populations, because, one may not be able to understand why a species is rare just by looking at how many offspring an organisms can produce. The same reasoning leads us to consider community ecology as a separate subdiscipline, as it may be impossible to understand the change in one population without understanding its interactions with other species. So, we have a hierarchy of ecological subdisciplines, because, nature is hierarchical and there are phenomena that are understood only when one studies the appropriate level within the hierarchy.

1.2 PHYSIOLOGICAL ECOLOGY

Density dependent influences change strength according to the density of individuals. Intraspecific competition is a good example of density dependent influence. Density independent influences have no relation to the density of individuals. It is best to think of these two influences as opposite ends of a continuum, as many factors are not strongly influenced by density, but are weakly density dependent or are density dependent only over a particular range of densities. The primary importance of density influence effects is the individual organisms interaction with the **abiotic** portion of its environment. Study of density influence effects is the field of **Physiological Ecology (= Autecology)**. A reminder that, although it is the individual that is the "unit" for physiological ecology and individuals of the same species vary, we will often treat a species as an individual.

The concepts of range and optimum deal with the individuals reaction to environmental variation. Assume that any abiotic factor which can affect the ecological performance of an individual will have **Range** of acceptable values. This differs from the range of possible values. It will also have **Optimum** at which the organism is most fit (in the evolutionary sense). It is possible for **multiple optima** to exist where there is a local peak in the performance of an individual. Multiple optima are more likely when species are considered, rather than individuals. Optimum can occur at any point in the range. It can even be at maximum or minimum for that range. However, this is rare. One should not get the impression that the optimum is midway between max and min. Example is measuring lizard's running speed at different temperatures. The optimal temperature is that temperature that maximizes running speed. **Intolerance** areas are areas which fall out of the individual's range. **Tolerance** is the ability to live and function under a particular set of conditions. **Physiological stress** is the gray area between intolerance and tolerance, where the animal pays some fitness cost. Often, physiological stress conditions are conditions that the individual can not endure indefinitely. Ecological stress must be measured in ecological terms, not in physiological terms. Cold might cause an endotherm (animal generating its own heat so that its body temperature is higher than its environment) to shiver—this is a physiological stress. If shivering uses up so much energy that the animal is more likely to die or is unable to devote as much energy to growth or reproduction, then the physiological stress becomes an ecological stress.

With respect to any factor some species (not individuals) will be **Stenotypic** and some will be Eurytypic. Stenotypic species will be able to tolerate a narrow range of that factor. **Eurytypic** species will be able to tolerate a wide range of that factor. These are relative terms and are best used for comparisons of the abilities of similar species.

1.3 COMMUNITY

When we use the term community in general, we do not mean simply all of the people living in a particular place. The term implies some interactions among the members and some greater unit than the individual. Same concept of community is used in ecology as well. Community is a collection of populations of different species all living in one place because the environment has the correct resources (food, etc.) and physical properties (temperature, etc.). In addition, a community has emergent properties dependent on the interaction of the populations living in it. The limits of a community are not easy to define and depend on the purpose of the ecologist defining the community.

Sometimes a community is all of the species occupying a particular habitat (this is the community definition relevant to discussing biomes). **Biomes** have been discussed in the next paragraph. Large scale systems (including all the species) have **trophic structure. Producers** of community produce biomass from energy derived from inorganic molecules and sunlight. Algae, plants and chemosynthetic bacteria are examples of producers. **Primary consumers** of community eat primary producers (also called herbivores). Algae grazers are primary consumers for example. **Secondary consumers** eat primary and other secondary consumers (also called predators). **Decomposers** catalyze complex organic detritus. Fungi feeding on leaf litter and scavengers are examples of decomposers. **Transformers** alter nutrients from inorganic to organic forms (or vice versa). Denitrifying bacteria and nitrifying bacteria are examples of transformers. Sometimes a community is a subset of the species occupying a particular habitat. It can be all the species at a particular trophic level (all of the plants in a field and all of the carnivores in a pond for example), or can be all of the species belonging to a taxonomic group (All of the yeast in the cactophilic habitat for example).

There are two basic categories of communities: terrestrial (land) and aquatic (water). These two basic types of community contain eight smaller units known as **biomes**. A biome is a large-scale category containing many communities of a similar nature, whose distribution is largely controlled by climate. Two broad classification of biomes is terrestrial biomes and aquatic biomes. Examples of terrestrial biomes are tundra, grassland, desert, taiga, temperate forest, and tropical forest. Examples of aquatic biomes are marine and freshwater. Major terrestrial biomes have been shown in Fig. 1.2.

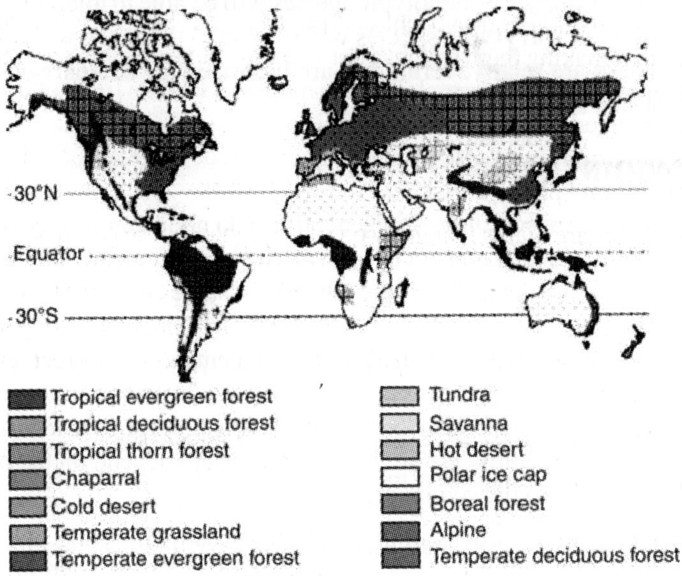

Fig. 1.2 Major terrestrial biomes

1.3.1 Terrestrial Biomes

Tundra and Desert

The tundra and desert biomes occupy the most extreme environments, with little or no moisture and extremes of temperature acting as harsh selective agents on organisms that occupy these areas. These two biomes have the fewest numbers of species due to the stringent environmental conditions. In other words, not everyone can live there due to the specialized adaptations required by the environment. Both have been discussed in detail later.

Tropical Rain Forests

Tropical rain forests occur in regions near the equator. The climate is always warm (between 20° and 25°C) with plenty of rainfall (at least 190 cm/year). The rain forest is probably the richest biome, both in diversity and in total biomass. The tropical rain forest has a complex structure, with many levels of life. More than half of all terrestrial species live in this biome. While diversity is high, dominance by a particular species is low.

While some animals live on the ground, most rain forest animals live on the trees. Many of these animals spend their entire life in the forest canopy. Insects are so abundant in tropical rain forests that the majority have not yet been identified. Charles Darwin noted the number of species found on a single tree, and suggested the richness of the rain forest would stagger the future systematist with the size of the catalogue of animal species found there. Termites are critical in the decomposition and nutrient cycling of wood. Birds tend to be brightly colored, often making them sought after as exotic pets. Amphibians and reptiles are well represented. Lemurs, sloths, and monkeys feed on fruits in tropical rain forest trees. The largest carnivores are the cats (jaguars in South America and leopards in Africa and Asia). Encroachment and destruction of habitat put all these animals and plants at risk.

Epiphytes are plants that grow on other plants. These epiphytes have their own roots to absorb moisture and minerals, and use the other plant more as an aid to grow taller. Some tropical forests in India, South-east Asia, West Africa, Central and South American are seasonal and have trees that shed leaves in dry season. The warm, moist climate supports high productivity as well as rapid decomposition of detritus.

With its yearlong growing season, tropical forests have a rapid cycling of nutrients. Soils in tropical rain forests tend to have very little organic matter since most of the organic carbon is tied up in the standing biomass of the plants. These tropical soils, termed laterites, make poor agricultural soils after the forest has been cleared.

About 17 million hectares of rain forest are destroyed each year (an area equal in size to Washington state). Estimates indicate the forests will be destroyed (along with a great part of the Earth's diversity) within 100 years. Rainfall and climate patterns could change as a result. Figure 1.3 shows typical tropical rain forest.

Fig. 1.3 Costa Rican cloud forest

Temperate Forests

The temperate forest biomes occur South of the Taiga in Eastern North America, Eastern Asia, and much of Europe. Rainfall is abundant (30-80 inches/year) and there is a well-defined growing season between 140 and 300 days. The Eastern United States and Canada are covered (or rather were once covered) by this biomes, natural vegetation. Dominant plants include beech, maple, oak; and other deciduous hardwood trees. Trees of a deciduous forest have broad leaves. They lose these leaves in the fall and grow again in the spring.

Sufficient sunlight penetrates the canopy to support a well-developed understory composed of shrubs, a layer of herbaceous plants, and then finally a ground cover of mosses and ferns. This stratification beneath the canopy provides a numerous habitats for a variety of insects and birds. The deciduous forest also contains many members of the rodent family. They serve as a food source for bobcats, wolves, and foxes. This area also is a home for deer and black bears. Winters are not as cold as in the taiga. Consequently, many amphibians and reptiles are able to survive (Fig. 1.4).

Fig. 1.4 Eastern deciduous forest

Shrubland (Chaparral)

The shrubland biome is dominated by shrubs with small but thick evergreen leaves. They are often coated with a thick, waxy cuticle, and with thick underground stems. As a result they survive the dry summers and frequent fires. Shrublands occur in parts of South America, Western Australia, central Chile, and around the Mediterranean Sea. Dense shrubland in California, where the summers are hot and very dry, is known as chaparral. This Mediterranean-type shrubland lacks an understory and ground litter, and is also highly flammable. The seeds of many species require the heat and scarring action of fire to induce germination (Fig. 1.5).

Fig. 1.5 Chaparral vegetation (predominantly Adenostema) in California

Grasslands

Grasslands occur in temperate and tropical areas with reduced rainfall (10-30 inches per year) or prolonged dry seasons. Grasslands occur in America, Africa, Asia, and Australia. Soils in this region are deep and rich. They are excellent for agriculture. Grasslands are almost entirely devoid of trees. They can support large herds of grazing animals. Natural grasslands once covered over 40 percent of the Earth's land surface. In temperate areas where rainfall is between 10 and 30 inches a year, grassland is the climax community. Reason is, because it is too wet for desert and too dry for forests.

Most grasslands have now been utilized to grow crops. Mostly it is wheat and corn. Grasses are the dominant plants, while grazing and burrowing species are the dominant animals. The extensive root systems of grasses allow them to recover quickly from grazing, flooding, drought, and sometimes fire.

Temperate grasslands include the Russian steppes, the South American pampas, and North American prairies. A tall-grass prairie occurs where moisture is not quite sufficient to support trees. A short-grass-prairie survives on less moisture and occurs between a tall-grass prairie and desert (Fig. 1.6).

Fig. 1.6 Short grass prairie, Nebraska

Animal life includes mice, prairie dogs, rabbits, and animals that feed on them (hawks and snakes for example). Prairies once also contained large herds of buffalo and pronghorn antelope. However, with human activity these once great herds have dwindled. The savanna is a tropical grassland that contains some trees. The savanna contains the greatest variety and numbers of herbivores (antelopes, zebras, and wildebeests, among others). This environment supports a large population of carnivores (lions, cheetahs, hyenas, and leopards). Any plant litter not consumed by grazers is attacked by termites and other decomposers. However, human activities are threatening this biomes. As a result, range for herbivores and carnivores is being reduced.

Deserts

Deserts are characterized by dry conditions (rainfall, usually less than 10 inches per year), and a wide temperature range. The dry air leads to wide daily temperature fluctuations from freezing at night to over 120 degrees during the day. Most deserts occur at latitudes of 30°N or S where descending air masses are dry. Some deserts occur in the rainshadow of tall mountain ranges or in coastal areas near cold offshore currents. Plants in this biome have developed a series of adaptations (such as succulent stems, absent leaves etc.) to conserve water and deal with these temperature extremes. Photosynthetic modifications are another strategy to life in the drylands.

The Sahara and a few other deserts have almost no vegetation. Most deserts, however, are home to a variety of plants. They are all adapted to heat and lack of abundant water (succulents and cacti for example). Animal life includes arthropods (especially insects and spiders), reptiles (lizards and snakes), running birds (the roadrunner of the American southwest and Warner Brothers cartoon fame), rodents (kangaroo rat and pack rat), and a few larger birds and mammals (hawks, owls and coyotes) (Fig. 1.7).

Fig. 1.7 Saguaro and cholla cacti in association with palo verde trees in the Sonoran desert, AZ

Taiga (Boreal Forest)

The taiga (pronounced "tie-guh") is a coniferous forest extending across most of the northern area of Northern Eurasia and North America. This forest belt also occurs in a few other areas, where it has different names. The taiga receives between 10 and 40 inches of rain per year and has a short growing season. Winters are cold and short, on the other hand, summers tend to be cool. The taiga is noted for its great stands of spruce, fir, hemlock, and pine. These trees have thick protective leaves and bark. The needlelike (evergreen) leaves can withstand the weight of accumulated snow. Taiga forests have a limited understory of plants, and a forest floor covered by low-lying mosses and lichens. Conifers, alders, birch and willow are common plants; wolves, grizzly bears, moose, and caribou are common animals. Dominance of a few species is pronounced. However, diversity is low when compared to temperate and tropical biomes (Fig. 1.8 and Fig. 1.9).

Fig. 1.8 Image of a Larix-dominated area of the taiga biomes

Fig. 1.9 Temperate rain forest, Washington

Tundra

The tundra covers the northernmost regions of North America and Eurasia, about 20% of the Earth's land area. This biome receives about 20 cm of rainfall annually. Snow melt makes water plentiful during summer months. Winters are long and dark, followed by very short summers. Water is frozen most of the time, producing frozen soil, permafrost. Vegetation includes no trees, but rather patches of grass and shrubs; grazing musk ox, reindeer, and caribou exist along with wolves, lynx, and rodents. A few animals highly adapted to cold live in the tundra year-round (lemming, ptarmigan for example). During the summer, the tundra hosts numerous insects and migratory animals. The ground is nearly completely covered with sedges and short grasses during the short summer. There are also plenty of patches of lichens and mosses. Dwarf woody shrubs flower and produce seeds quickly during the short growing season. The alpine tundra occurs above the timberline on mountain ranges, and may contain many of the same plants as the arctic tundra (Fig. 1.10).

Fig. 1.10 View of the tundra

Climate, Altitude and Terrestrial Biomes

Climate controls biome distribution by an altitudinal gradient and a latitudinal gradient. With increases of either altitude or latitude, cooler and drier conditions occur. Cooler conditions can cause aridity, since, cooler air can hold less water vapor than can warmer air.

Deserts can occur in warm areas due to a blockage of air circulation patterns that form a rain shadow (Figs. 1.11, 1.12 and 1.13).

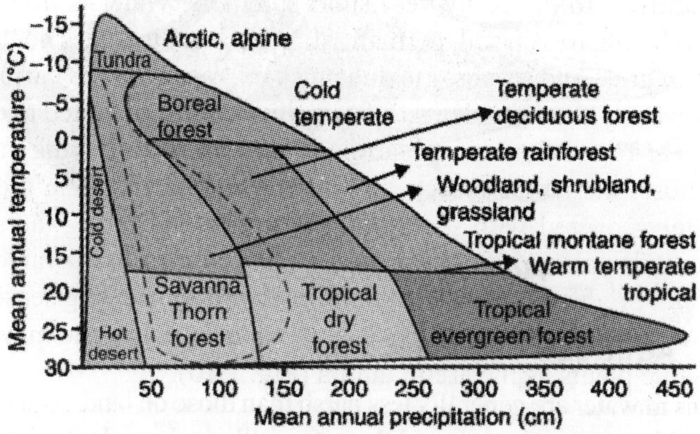

Fig. 1.11 Effect of temperature on precipitation

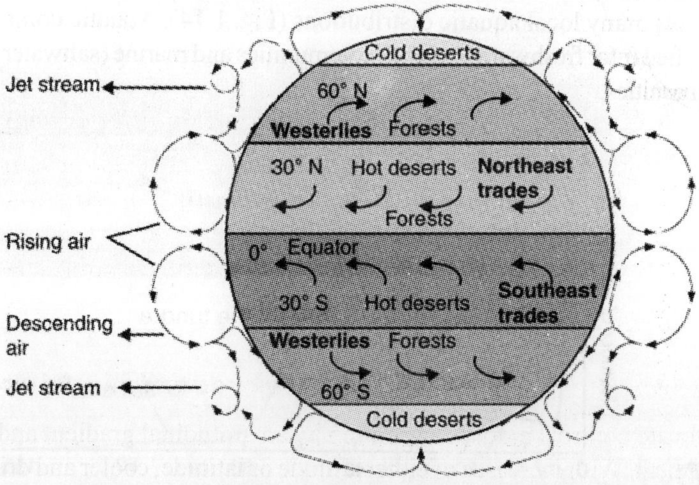

Fig. 1.12 Air circulation patterns and the global distribution of wet and dry areas

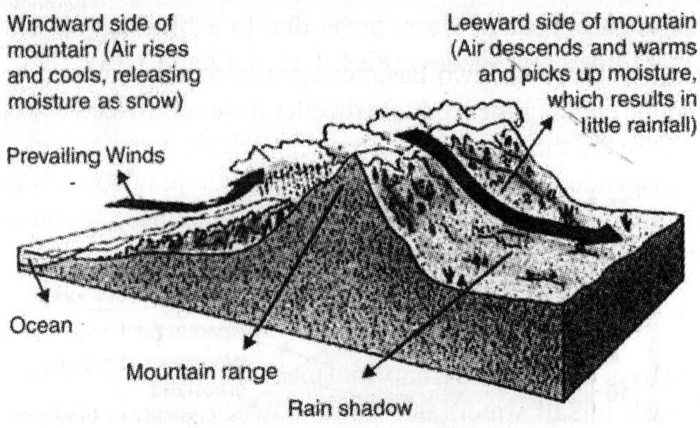

Fig. 1.13 Rain shadows and deserts

1.3.2 Aquatic Biomes

Conditions in water are generally less harsh than those on land. Aquatic organisms are buoyed by water support, and do not usually have to deal with desiccation. Despite covering 71% of the Earth's surface, areas of the open ocean are a vast aquatic desert containing few nutrients and very little life. Clearcut biome distinctions in water, like those on land, are difficult to make. Dissolved nutrients controls many local aquatic distributions (Fig. 1.14). Aquatic communities are classified into: freshwater (inland) communities and marine (saltwater or oceanic) communities.

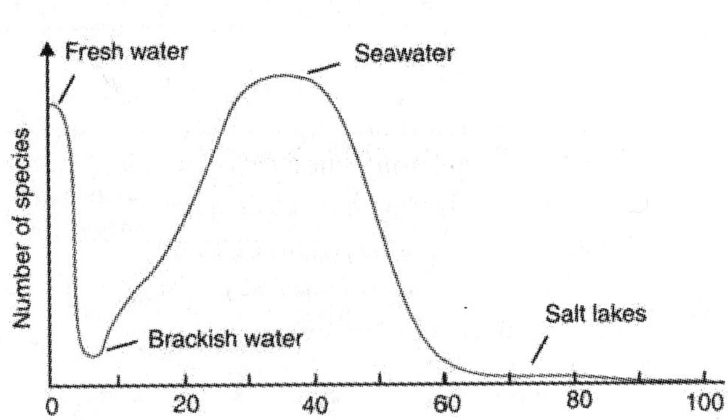

Fig. 1.14 Species diversity and salt concentration

The Marine Biomes

The marine biomes contain more dissolved minerals than the freshwater biomes. Over 70% of the Earth's surface is covered in water. Vast majority of that being saltwater. There are two basic categories to this biomes: benthic and pelagic. Benthic communities (bottom dwellers) are subdivided by depth. These subdivisions are the shore/shelf and deep sea. Pelagic communities (swimmers or floaters suspended in the water column) include planktonic (floating) and nektonic (swimming) organisms. The upper 200 meters of the water column is the euphotic zone. Light can penetrate to this zone.

Coastal Communities

Estuaries are bays where rivers empty into the sea. Erosion brings down nutrients and tides wash in salt water, and forms nutrient trap. Estuaries have high production for organisms that can tolerate changing salinity. They are called "nurseries of the sea" because many young marine fish develop in this protected environment.

Seashores

Rocky shorelines offer anchorage for sessile organisms. Seaweeds are main photosynthesizers and use holdfasts to anchor. Barnacles glue themselves to stone. Oysters and mussels attach themselves by threads. Limpets and periwinkles either hide in crevices or fasten flat to rocks.

Sandy beaches and shores are shifting strata. Permanent residents, therefore, burrow underground. Worms live permanently in tubes. Amphipods and ghost crabs burrow above high tide. Furthermore, they feed at night.

Coral Reefs

Areas of biological abundance in shallow, warm tropical waters. Stony corals have calcium carbonate exoskeleton. They may include algae as well most form colonies. They may associate with zooxanthellae dinoflagellates. Reef is densely populated with animal life. The Great Barrier Reef of Australia suffers from heavy predation by crown-of-thorns sea star. This probably is the reason that humans have harvested its predator, the giant triton.

Oceans

Oceans cover about three-quarters of the Earth's surface. Oceanic organisms are placed in either pelagic (open water) or benthic (ocean floor) categories. Pelagic division is divided into neritic and three levels of pelagic provinces. Neritic province has greater concentration of organisms, since, sunlight penetrates it. Nutrients are found here. Epipelagic zone is brightly lit. It has much photosynthetic phytoplankton, that support zooplankton that are food for fish, squid, dolphins, and whales. Mesopelagic zone is semi-dark. It contains carnivores, and adapted organisms tend to be translucent, red colored, or luminescent (shrimps, squids, lantern and hatchet fishes for example). Bathypelagic zone is completely dark and largest in size. It has strange looking fish. Benthic division includes organisms on continental shelf (sublittoral), continental slope (bathyal), and the abyssal plain.

Sublittoral zone harbors seaweed. It becomes sparse where deeper, is most dependent on slow rain of plankton and is detritus from sunlit water above. Bathyal zone continues with thinning of sublittoral organisms. Abyssal zone is mainly animals at soil-water interface of dark abyssal plain. In spite of high pressure, darkness and coldness, many invertebrates thrive here between sea urchins and tubeworms.

Thermal vents along oceanic ridges form a very unique community. Molten magma heats seawater to 350°C. It reacts with sulfate to form hydrogen sulfide (H_2S). Chemosynthetic bacteria obtain energy by oxidizing hydrogen sulfide. The resulting food chain supports a community of tubeworms and clams.

The Freshwater Biomes

The freshwater biome is subdivided into two zones: running water and standing water. Larger bodies of freshwater are less prone to stratification. Here oxygen decreases with depth. The upper layers have abundant oxygen. However, the lowermost layers are oxygen-poor. Mixing between upper and lower layers in a pond or lake occurs during seasonal changes. It is known as spring and fall overturn (Fig. 1.15).

Lakes are larger than ponds. They are stratified in summer and winter. The epilimnion is the upper surface layer. It is warm in summer. The hypolimnion is the cold lower layer. A sudden drop in temprature occurs at the middle of the thermocline. Layering prevents mixing between the lower hypolimnion (rich in nutrients) and the upper epilimnion (which has oxygen absorbed from its surface). The epilimnion warms in spring and cools in fall. It causes a temporary mixing. As a consequence, phytoplankton becomes more abundant due to the increased amounts of nutrients.

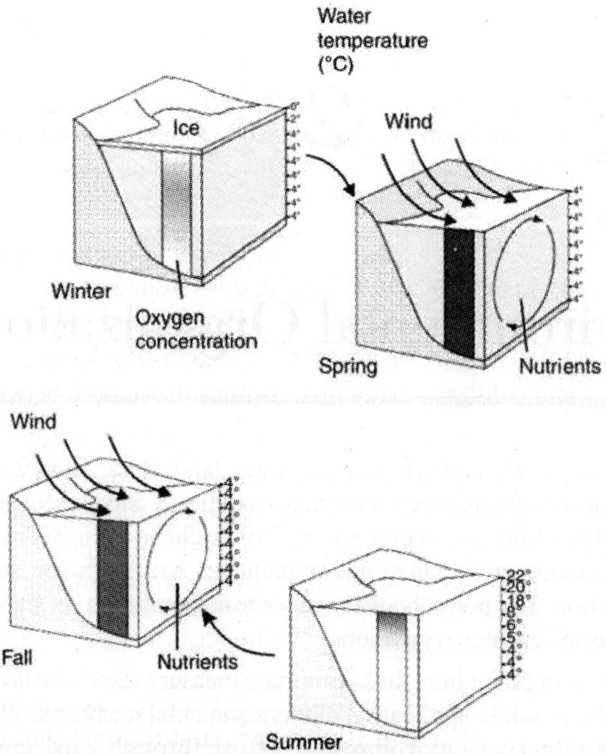

Fig. 1.15 Lake overturn

Life zones also exist in lakes and ponds. The littoral zone is closest to shore. The limnetic zone is the sunlit body of the lake. Below the level of sunlight penetration is the dark profundal zone. At the soil-water interface, we find the benthic zone. The term benthos is applied to animals that live on the bottom.

Rapidly flowing, bubbling streams have insects and fish adapted to oxygen-laden water. Slow moving streams have aquatic life more similar to lake and pond life.

REVIEW QUESTIONS

1. What is Ecology? Give detailed explanation. What are its subdisciplines?
2. Write short note on Physiological ecology.
3. Describe about following terrestrial biomes:
   (*i*) Tropical rain forests
   (*ii*) Shrubland
   (*iii*) Taiga
4. Enlist important aquatic biomes types.

2

Environmental Organization

The natural resources of the Earth like air, water, land, flora, fauna and natural eco-systems must be safeguarded for the benefit of future and present generation through careful planning and management. This could be achieved by creating a unified organizations which will handle air pollution, noise pollution, solid waste and water pollution. The body should have some authorities to set standards for implementation and enforce regulations.

Through this organization, the appropriate measure should be taken at any level to reach the possible application of environmental measures. We need to develop more effective environmental effort through this appropriate environmental organization.

2.1 ORGANIZATION

Organization can be defined as the pattern of work conduct when two or more people are involved in the same project which includes the proper checks and balances in both lateral and vertical lines of communication. The organization must be integrating and committing responsibilities.

Some valid definition of organization can be developed if it contains essential elements such as:

(*a*) Mission, objective or goals.

(*b*) Division of tasks which requires accomplishing identifiable work units or sections.

(*c*) Allocation of tasks or activities to individuals within the work units or sections.

(*d*) Assemblage of work units or sections into a hierarchy of control with proper chain of authority.

(*e*) Standardized systems and procedures for communications, control and measurement.

In developed countries of the world, it has already been recognized that appropriate organizational and legal measures must be taken for eliminating the air, water, noise and other environmental pollution. The organization of pollution control varies from country to country.

2.1.1 Viability of Organization

A viable organization is well managed internally and the viability of organization is its capacity to live. It does not have life in the same sense as a biological organism or manifestation of the life process of the individuals that constitute it. An analysis of organizations and their relationship to the environment should be helpful in determining the factors necessary for viability.

2.1.2 Organizations as Eco-systems

In the ecological view, a viable organization is one that succeeds in relationship with its environment and that satisfies its members through open interaction and exchange systems for greater organization outputs.

There are four important interrelated variables for human ecological system which are population, environment, organization and technology. These are related to one another in the organization. An organization and its environment forming an organizational ecosystem is as shown in Fig. 2.1.

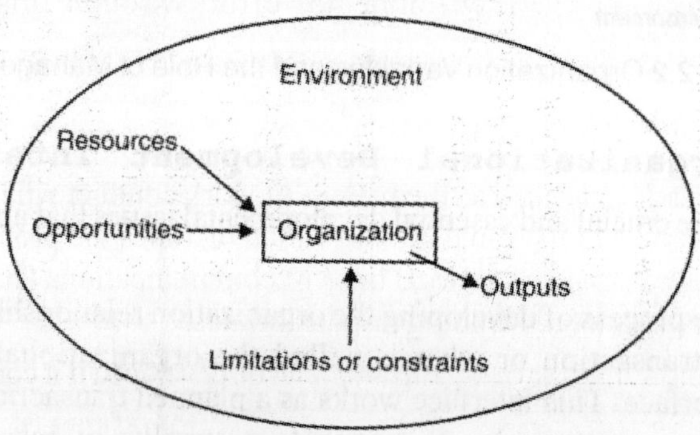

Fig. 2.1 An Organizational Eco-system

The environment provides resources, opportunities, and limitations for an organization. The output of an organization may be valued by its environment. For the development of new viable biological species, the two conditions are required. Firstly, it is mutation. The mutation may be a new product, process, procedure, policy, form or organization. The second condition is a favorable environment which permits new species or organization to live for the emergence and success of new biological species or organization.

2.1.3 Organization Variables

Organizations can be classified according to their goals or purposes, technology and structure. The ultimate goal of organization may not be identical with their output which are relevant and operational at all levels.

The technology of an organization includes not only the machinery, tools and equipment but also the specific human skills, knowledge and procedures used to operate these devices. Thus while technology does not fully determine organizational structure, it does not restrict choices among various ways of organizing.

The concept of structure employed here refers to the way in which departs or units are arranged within a system and linkage established among these. The key organizational characteristics are influenced by their environment and by one another and that they are satisfied with major factor which is role of management. This influence process is shown in Fig. 2.2.

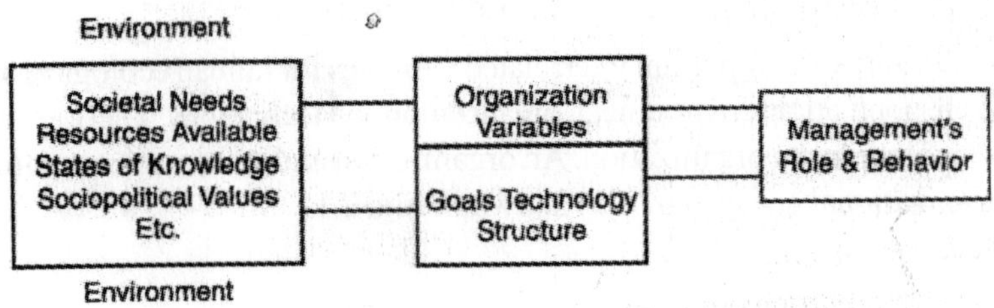

Fig. 2.2 Organization Variables and the Role of Management

2.1.4 Organizational Development Interface

There are three crucial and essential developmental issues that any organization faces:

(*a*) The process of developing the organization relationship or the nature of transaction or what is called the organizational environment interface. This interface works as a planned transaction to introduce the necessary idea to generate a surplus of resources for the organization.

(*b*) Planned transactions might involve a unique strategy for searching capital from the money markets or for securing technical sources.

Related to this basic issue is the proper division of activities which the organization finds necessary to carry out transactions with its environment. It is matter of different groups or units for the different kinds of activities which are required for execution of its selected transactional strategy.

(*c*) The third developmental issue is suggested by the definition of organization and has to do with the interface between individual founders. Once an organization is launched, it is transactional strategy that usually generates a need for additional contributions from people which are not initially associated with it. These contributors may be in roles as managers or professional employees.

2.1.5 Environmental Organizational Structure

The main purpose of organizational structure is to aid management by defining the lines of authority, the division of labour as well as responsibilities, and the unity of command along with direction. They serve as the crucial mediator between the individual and the entire society.

The organizational structure is not a rigid hierarchy which must be followed for effective management. As an organization grows; it will have an influential organizational structure different from the standard structure. A new organizational structure may be necessary to determine shortcomings of the original structure and present informal structure.

2.2 ENVIRONMENTAL ORGANIZATIONAL PROGRAMME

2.2.1 Scope of the Problem

As society moves towards higher stages of industrial development, environmental quality problems are not to the same because of continuously changing environmental situation. For this changing situation environmental organizational programmes must be flexible, adaptive and innovative. In the formulation of these programmes, four basic questions have to be answered.

1. **What and how much should be done?**

   The answers depend on the existing situations and on the forecast of future development in which technical agencies play a key role.

2. **How should it be done?**

   This question is concerned with technology and management which includes the identification and qualification of pollution sources, base line surveys, monitoring systems, etc.

3. **Who should do it?**

   An internal policy decision will be needed to decide who should implement the programmes and which agency should be involved.

4. **When should it be done?**

   The answer to this question depends on the intensity of the problems and the benefits to be derived from the programmes.

2.2.2 Organizational Programme Component

1. **Legislation:** To achieve the main purpose of an organization, it should have constitutional laws and regulations, the rights and duties of members, and those of the authorities. When drawing up new legislation, the organization should consult with the interested bodies, such as national authorities, local associations, local authorities, as well as professional and trade associations.

2. **Implementation plan:** An environmental organizational programme as a whole should be planned on the broadest scale to defense against unforeseen and unsuspected perils. Such programmes require appropriate monitoring and surveillance and the willingness to invest in research and development to develop implementation plans. The implementation plan should:
   - be simple and straightforward;
   - be capable of achieving its objectives;
   - be flexible and adaptable;
   - be realistic in terms of economics and social applications;
   - be subject to regulation, evaluation and change;
   - clearly define the responsibilities;
   - acknowledge the need for public support and give adequate provision for education;
   - recognize the need for research;
   - take into account differences among communities;
   - use standards that are practical and have been tested with qualitative aspects.

3. **Institutional and administrative arrangements:** Institutional and administrative arrangements are concept of managing human affairs to preserve biological health as well as diversity and ecological balance. This is interface between man's activity and nature.

   An important point to be considered with regard to arrangements is that one cannot be one's own judge. A number of institutional and administrative arrangements are concerned with coordination.

4. **Coordination:** The coordination largely depends on collaboration and cooperation of handling information. The coordination function must include communication with a variety of organization.

   Administrative capability is essential to all planning and coordination. Even in developed countries, lack of financial resources and of trained personnel sometimes constitutes a serious handicap in setting up efficient coordination system.

5. **Evaluation:** Evaluation is a process for analyzing results in relation to goods, for measuring benefits against costs and determining the relevance of programmes to environmental quality needs. The objectives of evaluation must be viewed within social context in which decisions are made, since, the resources available are always limited. Some of these objectives are:
   - clarification of social purposes and values;
   - clarification of objectives of programmes and organization;
   - validating of cause and effective relation for effective programmes.

   Evaluation provides information that is useful in planning and other decision making aspects in the form of conclusion and reference. Evaluation is more efficient programme for public participation.
6. **Resources:** The resources necessary to implement organizational programme contribute to social and economical development. Adequate resources must be available directly to environmental organizations.
7. **Financing:** Finance can come from public authorities or the private sector. The financing is complicated by other factors like the increasing costs of goods and services which is based on advanced technology and environmental quality standards and reluctance. The choice of method of financing is clearly influenced by political, social, and economical climate of the community. It is from public funds, taxes, levies or user charges.
8. **Manpower:** It is essential to have high grade professional officers with both technical and administrative training to develop and implement these programmes in both industrialized and developing countries with knowledge of various aspects of environmental quality control. The number of officers depends on the size of organization and scope of the problems.
9. **Programme constraints:** The constraints must be identified and evaluated at the planning stage and taken into account in the formulation of the programme. These constraints are concerned with the delivery of services to the public. Some constraints result from geographical or climatic conditions. These are:
   (*a*) *Inadequate scientific knowledge:* The lack of knowledge is a serious obstacle to the establishment of environmental quality standards and the setting of the programme priorities. Other considerations are inadequate technology and inadequate resources.

   (*b*) *Unsuitable administrative and organizational framework.*

(c) *Social factors:* Lack of social awareness and understanding of the problems by the public may be an important reason for the low priority accorded to environmental quality control.

(d) *Political constraints:* Environmental quality control programmes may be politically desirable or inopportune because of the restrictions on economic development. Decisions on economic development schemes should be made with reference to environmental consequences which affect the health of man and the ecology.

2.2.3 Support Programmes

1. **Education and information:** The environmental organizations should emphasize the need for education on environmental quality control at all levels of the community. Environmental education programmes should both inform and influence the public, convincing them of the importance of prevention. A service should be developed to encourage the public participation in environmental quality control programmes by considering the publics' comments and suggestions.
2. **Research:** To solve existing environmental quality problems to prevent future hazards, research is necessary. Research and development programme covering all environmental quality programme and exchange of research information between an organization is therefore essential.

2.3 RESPONSIBILITIES AND FUNCTIONS OF AN ENVIRONMENTAL ORGANIZATION

The most important responsibilities and functions of an organization are:

2.3.1 Policy Formulation

The environmental organizations should develop firm policies appropriate to its goals. They must fit into the political and administrative framework in which they will be implemented. An important problem in making policy decisions has to be continuously answered in the determination of these priorities:

- How serious the consequences of the environmental problems are likely to be?
- How widespread will they be?
- How immediate they will be?
- To what extent will they be reversible and what will be the probable cost?

- What is the cost of avoiding the problem in relation to the benefits to be achieved?

2.3.2 Setting Standards

Environmental standards should be established to safeguard the environment. They should not be aimed at gaining trade advantages and should be realistic. Criteria for the rational and scientific foundations for the standards are based on administrative decisions and actions. Criteria documents should be strictly scientific in nature.

2.3.3 To Carry Out and to Coordinate

Various programmes and activities are to be carried out and be coordinated to achieve the organizations goals, such as:

1. **Implementation plans.**
2. **Institutional and administrative arrangements.**
3. **Investigations, studies and research:** The environmental organizations should promote investigations, studies and researches so as to provide the best information in the form of criteria document and to establishment of environmental quality standards.
4. **Monitoring and surveillance:** Monitoring programmes are concerned with sources of pollutant levels in environmental media, and the effect of the pollutants. The essential components of monitoring and surveillance programmes are:
   - Compilation, analysis and evaluation of relevant data in terms of the available criteria and standards.
   - The application of measures indicated by these findings.
   - A feedback mechanism to facilitate the updating of scientific and technological knowledge.

   Monitoring and surveillance programmes may be initiated for several reasons:
   - For environmental quality management to establish the standards.
   - To deal with the scientific pollution problem over a wider geographical area.
   - To develop more sensitive techniques to identify a new pollutant.
   - To determine pollution trends.
   - To device model of human exposure.

   Monitoring and surveillance programmes require many resources in terms of professional experts, equipment and facilities, time and costs to determine priorities to be monitored. The second most important steps are the specification of sampling requirements, measurements methods and instruments and data processing and evaluating procedures.

5. **Guide and information:** A relevant guide and information must be supplied to the public to avoid the risk or significant adverse effects on the environment. A service should be developed to encourage public participation in organizational programmes which considers the public comments and suggestions. Such an arrangement would facilitate:
   - The dissemination and interpretation of factual information to the public.
   - The development of extension programmes aimed at creating a better understanding by the public of basic environmental problems and programmes.
   - The availability of environmental material suitable for use in the schools.
6. **Evaluation.**

2.4 VARIOUS ORGANIZATIONS IN ENVIRONMENT RELATED FIELDS

The following statements summarize the various organizations in environmental related fields:

2.4.1 International Level

1. **The United Nations:** The United Nations secretariat, the specialized agencies and regional economic commissions are all concerned with environmental problems. It has following units to handle environmental problems.

   (*a*) *The secretariat*: Environmental questions are handled within UN secretariat in the department of economic and social affairs and involve the following units :
   - The office of science and technology to utilize the natural resources.
   - The social department division for regional planning, and development as well as utilization of human resources.
   - The center for housing, building and planning to prevent the deterioration of the human environment due to urban sprawl, noise, air, and water pollution, traffic congestion, etc.

– The resources and transport division for difficult trade offs.

– Public administration division for study of administrative aspects of urbanization.

(*b*) *The United Nations development programme*: It is helped to finance a large number of resource surveys, projects related to conservation, studies of ecological changes as a result of the creations large manmade bodies of water and training programmes.

(*c*) *The United Nations scientific committee on the effects of atomic radiation*: This is established in 1955 to concern about radioactive fall out from nuclear weapon testing.

2. The specialized and affiliated agencies: They are as follows:

(*a*) *The international labour organization*: The organization is concerned with occupation health and hazards to prevent dust in mining, travelling and quarrying and in air pollution control in industrial development.

(*b*) *The food and agricultural organization*: It is deeply involved in the conservation of soil, forests, and terrestrial waters.

(*c*) *United nations educational, scientific and cultural organization*: Its creation is concerned with environmental issues. It is known as **UNESCO**. It has conducted and simulated in cooperation with other interested organizations to solve the scientific problems of the environment. It is related to education, social science, culture and information as well as science and also study the behavioral factors of natural sciences.

(*d*) *United nations environment programmes.*

(*e*) *World health organization (WHO)*: It is focused on three aspects which are as follows:

– The definition of environmental standards including research designed to establish the limits of human adaptability to various stress factors.

– The identification of environmental hazards and the effects of pesticides, the ecology and biology of disease factors, the abuse of drugs and maize.

– The study of the effect of induced changes in the environment, such as rapid population changes, mass migration, urbanization, and the construction of irrigation dams and man-made lakes.

(*f*) *World meteorological organization (WMO)*: It is engaged in the development of a world weather watch based on an international monitoring system. It studies the relationship of air pollutants meteorology and plant damage and works with international atomic energy agency.

(*g*) *International maritime consultative organization (IMCO)*: It is responsible for the safety of ships and for preventing pollution of the land, sea or air by or from ships, vessels and other equipments operating in marine environment. It is also dealing with spillages, including the carriage of oil and other noxious and hazardous cargoes.

(*h*) *International atomic energy agency (IAEA)*: It studies and provides technical assistance on radioactive pollution of all environments, and problems involving storage and disposal of radioactive wastes.

(*i*) *International civil aviation organization (ICAO)*: It concern with the human environment centres on two subjects such as aircraft noise and the problem of the sonic boom.

3. **The UN regional economic commissions:** It involves:
   - The economic and social commissions for Asia and the pacific.
   - The economic commission for Latin America.
   - The economic commission for Africa.
   - The economic commission for Europe.
4. **Other organizations:** Outside the UN system, other organizations such as:
   - The World Bank.
   - The council of Europe.
   - The organization for economic cooperation and development.
   - The north Atlantic treaty organization.
   - The organization for African unity.
   - The national academy of science.
   - Ford foundation, etc.

2.4.2 National Level

A few generalizations could be put forward in national level:

(*a*) Concerns about environmental degradation of highly industrialized world.

(*b*) In the developing world, a number of governments had come to conclusion that they were in trouble with the natural systems.

Typical environmental organizations at national levels are as follow:

1. **The United States:**

   (*a*) *The council of environmental quality (CEQ)*: The duties and functions of the council are as follows:

   - To assist and advise the president in the preparation of environmental quality reports.
   - To gather timely and authorised information regarding conditions and trends in the quality of the environment both current and prospective to analyze and interpret the information.
   - To review and appraise the various programmes and activities.
   - To develop and recommend to the President, national policies to foster and promote the improvement of environmental quality.
   - To conduct investigations, studies, surveys, research and analyses relating to ecological systems and environmental quality.
   - To document and define changes in the natural environment, including the plant and animal systems and to accumulate necessary data and other information.
   - To report at least once each year to the president on the state and condition of the environment.
   - To make and furnish such studies, reports and recommendations with respect to policy and legislation.

   (*b*) *The environmental protection agency (EPA)*: The following activities are transferred to the EPA such as:

   - Functions of the federal water quality administration.
   - Functions regarding pesticides.
   - Functions of the national air pollution control agency.
   - Functions of the bureau of solid waste management and bureau of water hygiene.
   - Functions respecting radiation criteria.
   - Authority to perform studies of ecological systems.

2. **Thailand:** At present, the Thai government is already aware of waste water pollution and solid waste problems in metropolitan and industrial estates. The following discussion summarizes the different organizations and their functions in relation to environmental management.

(*a*) *National energy authority*: Heat recovery and electric generation from incineration of refuse and solid wastes.

(*b*) *Ministry of industry*: Sets standards for industrial effluents and construction of waste treatment plants.

(*c*) *Environmental health division, ministry of public health*: Conducts research on the deterioration of streams and rivers and effect of pollution on human health.

(*d*) *National environmental board*: Established to evaluate projects of governmental agencies and state private enterprises which may have adverse effects on environmental quality.

3. **Malaysia:** In Malaysia, the division of environment (DOE) is established under the ministry of science and technology. The DOE is headed by a director general who is assisted by three directors which are director of air quality management, pollution control and director of administration.

4. **Philippines:** In Philippines, a national environmental protection council (NEPC) was created on April 1977 which is under the supervision and control of the President of Philippines. The major power and function of the council are:
   - Environment or environment related laws and coordination of environmental protection research.
   - To formulate policies for environmental quality standards and environmental impact assessment.
   - To undertake research programmes monitoring projects and conduct public hearings.
   - To conduct educational and training campaign.
   - To prepare annual environment status reports.

2.5 SUMMARY

Better environmental protection can be achieved if unified organization can be created to handle air pollution, water pollution, solid wastes and noise pollution. This organization should have the authority to impose effluent, influent and process standards to set target dates for implementation of standards, impose fines, discharge charges, penalties and recommend legislation pertaining to environmental quality.

The environmental organizational programmes should emphasize the need for public participation in decisions concerning environmental quality.

Education in environmental matters is essential in order to broaden the basis for an enlightened opinion of individuals, enterprises, and communities in protecting and improving the environment.

National environmental pollution control programmes should be designed to ensure adequate pollution control and abatement. For long term, we need much more knowledge of values of environmental problems and we need to move aggressively to deal with the problems that can be dealt within knowledge and by existing institutions.

Without such a systematic approach, the current piecemeal, unrelated efforts will achieve only partial and unsatisfactory progress in meeting the environmental problems of tomorrow.

REVIEW QUESTIONS

1. Define organization. What are its essential elements? Justify it as eco-system.
2. Describe about organizational programme components.
3. Enlist important responsibilities and functions of an environmental organization.
4. What is the role of the following organizations in environmental related fields:
   (*i*) The United Nations
   (*ii*) EPA of United States
   (*iii*) National level environmental organization of Thailand.

3

Environmental Impact Assessment

3.1 INTRODUCTION

3.1.1 The Concept of Environment

Broader interpretation of the term 'environment' has been provided by the National Environmental Policy Act (NEPA) of USA. According to this, the term 'environment' includes physical, social, cultural, economic and aesthetic dimensions. We may say that the term or concept of environment means the whole complex of physical including chemical, social, cultural, economic, and aesthetic factors which affect individuals and communities and ultimately determine their form, character, relationship and survival. A complete description of the environment by considering all such factors is denoted by the term 'environmental inventory'. Any natural or man-made change in the environment such as air pollution, land-use patterns, deforestation, excessive rise in population, technological changes, earthquakes, cyclones, drifting of mountains, rise in sea levels, etc. will eventually affect the living-beings and change their life-styles or patterns of behavior and survival.

The different dimensions of environment have a number of categories of factors or elements. Some of them are as follows:

(*i*) **Physical Environment:** This includes the physical, chemical, and biological factors, both natural as well as man-made. Major elements in this category are:

(*a*) *Land and Climate*: General conditions of soils, geology, topography, sub-surface conditions, special conditions like flood-plain, landslides, earthquakes, climatic conditions, etc.

(*b*) *Vegetations, Wildlife and Natural Areas*: This includes all biological elements including special natural areas for species. Emphasis will be on factors like extent and type of vegetation and wildlife, existence of unique natural systems such as streams, wildlife breeding areas, forest, and wilderness areas on the site and nearby it.

(*c*) *Surrounding land-uses and Physical Character of the Area*: This includes various types of developments such as single family or high rise residential, industrial and commercial buildings, open spaces, population density, housing density, industrial and commercial footage per acre of land, building designs, etc.

(*d*) *Infrastructure*: Public services factors such as water supply systems, sewage systems, energy resources, transportation systems, and communication facilities, etc.

(*e*) *Air Pollution Levels*: Partly this comes under climatic conditions. But because of human activities the extent of air pollution may change which is to be taken into account.

(*f*) *Noise Pollution Sources*: Such as nearby railway, airport, highway, factories, markets, etc.

(*g*) *Water Pollution Levels*: Various sources of water such as ground water, surface water, and quality of water for general and specific uses, sources of water pollution and water-treatment facilities; waste and storm water disposal facilities, etc.

(ii) **Social Environment:** This will include a large number of factors or elements related to social and cultural life of people. Populations and its density, community composition, social cohesion, educational factors, religions, norms, values, sanctions governing the people, family structure, politics, etc. will be quite predominating factors which define social environment. Community facilities and services like schools, parks, hospitals, recreation and cultural facilities, etc. will also be included in this category.

(iii) **Economic Environment:** This includes all economic factors such as employment and unemployment levels, levels and sources of income, economic base of the area and its surrounding, availability of critical factors of production, demand patterns, land values, taxes, economic administration, trade, etc.

(iv) **Aesthetic Environment:** This sub-category is comprised of the factors which we call as significantly values historical, archeological or architectural objects or sites; scenic areas, views and landscapes.

3.1.2 Environmental Impact Assessment

The EIA (Environmental Impact Assessment) is an activity designed to identify and predict the impacts on bio-geographical environment and on man's health and well-being of legislature proposals, policies, programmes, projects and operational procedures, and to interpret and communicate information about the impacts. The EIA exercise gives recognition to the fact that environmental considerations related to the projects, programmes and other actions are important and so they are to be incorporated in the decision-making process. An industrial project may be quite sound in generating very high profits but may pollute water or air causing very high social cost. Through EIA, we consider all aspects of the projects, plans, programmes and legislative actions relative to the physical, chemical, biological, cultural and socioeconomic components of the total environment.

Environmental impacts may be ‘primary’ or ‘direct’ and ‘secondary’ or ‘indirect’. The primary impacts are in fact the first round impacts associated with projects, programmes and other activities of man such as air pollution, water pollution, noise, employment generation, displacement of people and businesses, etc. Construction of highways, airports, dams, power houses and other large projects would generate several types of primary impacts. Normally, a project’s inputs cause ‘primary’ impacts and its outputs cause ‘secondary’ impacts. Most of the socioeconomic environmental changes fall in the category of ‘secondary’, i.e. induced effects or impacts.

Environmental impacts may also be classified as ‘short-term’ and ‘long-term’. The impacts which are felt in the shorter period of time such as during construction period of a project and its early phase of operation, or of an action when it becomes operative are short-term in nature. The impacts which are felt in a longer period of time are defined as ‘long-term’ impacts. Economists take a time period over which certain factor of production is fixed, i.e. unchanged as a short-term and when all factors of production including the size of the plant is variable then it is a long-term impact. Construction noise, dusting, traffic disruption, air pollution, water pollution, removal of forests, displacement of people, shifting of businesses, etc. are some examples of the short-term environmental impacts. Pollution from the use of septic systems, poor drainage, infrastructural overcrowding, growth inducing effects, disruption or improvements in social cohesion, changes in cultural values, changes in economic structure, rise in sea-level, drifting of mountains, drying-up of rivers, changes in the pattern of climate, etc. are some examples of the long-term environmental impacts.

Considering the nature of the short-term and long-term environmental impacts, positive or negative, one may find a trade-off between them. A project like Narmada dam in India may displace people in the short-term, submerge a large tract of forest and create all kinds of construction damages, but it brings economic prosperity in the long run. The green revolution in the short-term improves farm productivity and hence incomes of farmers, but in the long run, one may find a declining fertility of farms due to excessive use of chemicals used as fertilizers and insecticides. Through proper environmental impact analysis one may get a clear idea of such trade-offs and suggest appropriate mitigation measures to minimize them.

Environmental changes might be natural and/or man-made. Natural changes might be 'irreversible' (like mountain building, eutrophication of a lake) or 'cyclic' (e.g. changes in annual weather) or 'transient' (e.g. droughts). Man's uses of fire, domestication of animals, introduction of agriculture in place of hunting, industries and development of high levels of technological processes, large human settlements, fast moving modes of transportation and communication, invention and use of chemicals, etc. are some examples of man-made environmental changes.

A broad version of the environmental impact assessment (EIA) is defined by Lee and Walsh (1992) as the strategic environmental assessment (SEA) which is applied to policies, plans or programmes. It is in fact a programmatic EIA applied at the higher levels of decision making hierarchy, i.e. regional or state of national levels. At the local level it will be applied to projects and, therefore, is analogous to the EIA. A country makes policies at the national level from which action plans are drawn at the national, state or regional levels. SEA is relevant for these types of activities but finally at the local level a tangible shape to the policies/actions will be given through projects.

3.1.3 Significant Environmental Impacts

What should be the criteria for identification of the 'significant impacts'? Normally, three bases are used for this purpose. These are:

(*i*) significance based on institutional recognition or requirements;

(*ii*) significance based on public recognition;

(*iii*) significance based on technical considerations.

The institutional recognition takes into account public laws, executive orders, rules and regulations, treaties and other policy statements of the Central and State governments related to the maintenance of the environmental quality. Such provisions cannot be violated. By 'public recognition' we mean that some segments of the general public recognize the importance of environment, although there might be no government law to protect it. Normally, we see controversies, protests, and agitation, etc. from public on several environmental issues related to projects or actions of government or private parties.

The third category, i.e. significance based on technical recognition implies that environmental quality is to be maintained based on scientific or technical knowledge or judgment of the critical resources. For example, environmental quality of Antarctic is to be maintained, because, it provides a good setting for scientific study of geological formation, climate and other related aspects.

Haug et al. (1984) designed a structural scheme to identify significance of environmental impacts on the basis of a probability of their crossing the threshold level of concern. Threshold priorities as suggested by them are:

(i) **High Priorities Legal Threshold:** These are established by law or regulation. They should not be exceeded in any circumstance.

(ii) **Very High Priority Functional Threshold:** These are established for resource uses and adverse environmental impacts. If these threshold limits are exceeded, the functioning of the economic system will be disturbed sufficiently to destroy the resources and biosphere of the nation.

(iii) **High Priority Normative Thresholds:** These are established for resource uses on the basis of social norms at local or regional levels.

(iv) **Moderate Priority Controversial Thresholds:** Such thresholds of impacts or resource uses are generally controversial. They may be source of conflicts between various individuals or groups of people. For example, Tehri Hydroelectric Power Project.

(v) **Low Priority Preference Threshold:** Such threshold when exceeded may be questionable to some individuals on the basis of their preferences but not to the society as a whole. That is why they are assigned low priority.

Keeping in mind the above discussion, one may identify the significant environmental impacts associated with projects or actions. Environmental laws, regulations, policies or executive orders, political or public considerations, and scientific or technical considerations are taken into account to identify such impacts. National and State Governments would be playing a pivotal role in protective the environment. They provide the guidelines and thresholds or 'standards' for maintenance of the environment in order to provide a clean and living human environment.

3.1.4 The Stages of Environmental Impact Analysis

There are four broad levels or stages for environmental impact analysis or assessment: 'local level', 'regional level', 'national level' and 'global level' or stage. Some effects or impacts of a project or action will be confined to the location or site of the project or action. A study of such effects or impacts would constitute the local level EIA. There will be some effects which spread over a wider area around the project. Such impacts are analyzed under 'regional level' EIA. When the whole country is affected by the project or action then the EIA level will be 'national' and when the entire world is affected as in the case of ozone layer depletion, then it will be global EIA. Between 'national' and 'global' stages, we may have 'international' level EIA as a part of the global level. For example, forest depletion in Nepal may affect the climate and stream water outflow in India and Bangladesh. It requires international cooperation to study such impacts.

3.1.5 Environmental Impacts and Stages of Development

The perception of environmental impacts to a great extent depends on the degree of economic development of the countries and/or individuals. In less developed countries, we find widespread poverty. A large number of people in these countries do not have adequate quantity of food to eat, shelter to live, medical facilities for treatment, education for skill development and old age security, etc. Poor quality of environment is tolerated in these countries, because, the focus of the people is on quantity of goods and services and not on their quality. This situation is often termed as 'Pollution of Poverty'.

In the developed countries, as we see, there is no shortage of the life supporting goods and services. In fact, sometimes there is a surplus of them. People in such countries are quality conscious. They may face environmental pollution due to 'too much development'. Technology, typical consumption patterns, social tensions, and several other factors might cause environmental pollution which is often termed as 'Pollution of Affluence'. Both the types of environmental pollution are to be avoided, but how to do this is a major problem before the world. International co-operation will be helpful in this context.

3.2 MEASUREMENT OF ENVIRONMENTAL IMPACTS

3.2.1 Impact Assessment Methods

The process of environmental impact assessment involves several stages like identification of environmental indicators and their impacts on man and ecology, measurement of impacts, prediction and interpretation of impacts, evaluation of alternatives and finally communicating the impacts. There might be differences in measurement techniques, interpretation of impacts and so the decision maker faces the problem of the choice of the method to do all the above mentioned activities of EIA in the most 'equitable' way.

There are some specific characteristics which an EIA methodology should depict. These are: (*a*) it should be appropriate to the necessary task of the EIA process such as impact identification or comparison of alternatives; (*b*) it should be significantly free from assessor's bias; (*c*) it should be economical in terms of costs, and its requirement of data, investigating time, personnel, equipment and facilities.

There is no universal 'methodology' of EIA so far, which shows all the above mentioned characteristics and which can be applied to all project types in all environmental settings. Warner (1973) divided all available methods into 5 main categories namely: (*a*) 'ad hoc', (*b*) overlay techniques; (*c*) checklists, (*d*) matrices and (*e*) networks.

Ad Hoc Methods

These are very simple methods based on subjective or intuitive assessment of environmental impacts on broad aspects. A team of specialists depending on their areas of expertise would provide minimum guidance without going into detailed scientific investigation of environmental impacts of projects and other actions. The impacts and their types such as short-term and/or long-term, reversible or irreversible, etc. are examined merely on guess basis. Opinion polls, experts opinion, Delphi methods, etc. all come in category of ad hoc methods of environmental impact assessment. Such methods are quite poor.

Checklist Methods

Such methods are basically a variant of the ad hoc methods. However, they are quite elaborative and involve systematic assessment of the environmental impacts of projects and other activities. Checklist means a listing of potential environmental impacts. Preparation of such a list is the first step of the method. The listing is normally done category-wise, i.e. in structured form. It may be a 'simple checklist', i.e. no information is given about data requirement, measurement or impacts predication, and 'descriptive checklist' which gives data measurement and prediction details also. The second step of EIA by using the checklist method is to assess the nature of the impact, i.e. its type such as adverse or beneficial, short-term or long-term, no effect or significant impact, reversible or irreversible, etc. To identify such impact types, the normal practice is to put a cross mark 'X' under the identified type or types against each impact area or domain. A simple abstract example is given below for this in Table 3.1.

Table 3.1 Environmental Areas vs Types of Impacts

Environmental Area	No Effect	Positive Effect	Negative Effect	Direct	Indirect	Short-term	Long-term
Wildlife			X			X	
Air Pollution			X	X			
Water Pollution		X				X	
Noise			X			X	
Economic Value		X		X			X
Public Health				X			

The crosses 'X' can simply be counted and appropriate conclusions can be derived from them. Sometimes 'weights' can be assigned to the environmental indicators or areas to make the processes of EIA much more useful.

Construction of checklist is a very cumbersome task. In fact, a single general checklist of impact areas with applicability to all projects and environmental conditions may be too large and not necessary. So checklists are prepared keeping in mind the type of projects or actions and objectives of the study. The 'screening' and 'scooping' stages of EIA will focus the issue of the EIA and the identification of the significant impacts for assessment.

Overlay Method

The method relies on a set of maps of a project area's environmental characteristics covering physical, social, ecological, aesthetic aspects. The maps (or transparencies) are then overlaid to produce a comprehensive description of the area's environment. Impacts are then identified by comparing the area's characteristics with a larger area or region as a whole. Computer programmes can be used to overlay the maps and thus arrive at the conclusions regarding environmental impacts of the project in the concerned location. The recent technique of the remote-sensing through electromagnetic rays is increasingly being used for this purpose although it is costly.

Matrix Method

This method and its variants provide us a framework of interaction of different actions or activities of a project with potential environmental impacts caused by them. A 'simple interaction matrix' is formed where project actions are listed along one axis, say, vertically downward and environmental impacts are listed on the other axis, say, horizontally. Such a matrix allows us to identify the cause-effect relationships between various actions and the environmental impacts associated with them. It has also been extended further in the form of 'stepped matrix' to take care of 'cross impacts', i.e. impacts in subsequent rounds induced by the first round impacts. We will concentrate only to the 'simple matrix' technique in this analysis.

Leopold et al. matrix for assessing environmental impacts is fairly exhaustive. This matrix lists about 100 project actions and about 88 environmental 'characteristics' and 'conditions'. The process for the use of the matrix for assessing environmental impacts is very simple. The process starts with identification of all actions that are parts of the proposed project. Impacts of these actions are then identified, and the matrix is marked with a diagonal line in the appropriate interaction place.

The second step in using the Leopold matrix is to describe the impact interaction in terms of its magnitude and importance. 'Magnitude' of an interaction is its extensity, marked in terms of a number from 1 to 10, where 10 represents a large magnitude and 1 a small magnitude.

The 'importance' weights are then assigned to the impacts by anticipating them. The scale of importance also varies from 1 to 10, where 10 represents a severe impact of highest importance while 1 represents a very low importance. Assignment of importance weights (1 to 10) will be based on subjective judgment of the individuals, small groups or inter disciplinary team working on the assessment study. The third step is then to sum the products of the 'magnitude' and 'importance' ranks across the rows and columns of the matrix. All rows sum or columns sum will give us an overall measurement of the impact score for the project.

Additional refinement in impact assessment with the help of the Leopold matrix can be made to identify beneficial as well harmful impacts through the use of appropriate designators such as plus and minus signs. The matrix can also be used to identify impacts at various time-bound (temporal) phases of a project, such as construction, operation, and post operation phases. It is also applied to describe impacts associated with various locations such as at the site, and in the region.

Let,

m_{ij} = (+ or –) magnitude of jth action on i^{th} environmental factor

W_{ij} = 'importance' weight of the jth action on i^{th} environmental factor

Both are in ranks as described earlier.

Total impact on i^{th} environmental factor = $\sum_j m_{ij} w_{ij}$, $i = 1$ to n.

Total impact of jth action on all environmental factor = $\sum_i m_{ij} w_{ij}$, $j = 1$ to n.

$$\text{Total impact score} = \sum_{i}^{n}\sum_{j}^{n} m_{ij} w_{ij}$$

Let us take an abstract hypothetical example to explain the procedure. In Table 3.2, a matrix of 7 environmental impacts against 5 project 'actions' is given. The entries contain the product of magnitude ranks and 'importance' weights in the form X(Y), where X= rank of magnitude of the impact and Y its 'importance' rank. A row-sum provide total impact on an environmental condition by all 'actions' and a column-sum gives the sum of impacts on all conditions by an action.

Table 3.2 Weighted Impacts of Project Actions (Hypothetical Entries)

Proposed Actions	Habitat Construction	Noise Variations	Impounding Water (Reservoir/ Dams)	Dredging	Fertilizer Use	Total Factor Impact
Environmental Conditions						
Land Form	5(3)		1(3)	1(1)	2(2)	23
Water	4(4)		3(4)	–2(3)	–3(3)	13
Forest	–2(2)		–4(2)	–3(2)	4(1)	–14
Wildlife	–3(2)	–2(3)	–3(2)			–24
Air Quality	1(4)		1(4)		–1(1)	07
Health	3(5)	–4(4)	2(5)		–2(4)	01
Economic Value	6(6)	2(5)	6(6)	3(5)	5(6)	127
Total Action Impact	76	–12	51	04	20	133

As the above table shows, total weighted impact score for the project is 133 which implies that on the whole it is beneficial. There are several negative impacts particularly on wildlife which are to be mitigated through proper devices.

An important application of the matrix method is to evaluate alternatives from the point of view of decision-making. Consider the following Table 3.3.

Highway alternatives are shown on tops of the columns and environmental impacts on rows beginning.

Table 3.3 Selection of a Highway Route

Impact Area (*)	**Highway 1**	**Alternatives 2**	**(Actions) 3**	**4**
Market Access Time (Rank)	25(4)	18(3)	14(1)	17(2)
Level of Service (Rank)	50(1)	45(2)	40(4)	42(3)
Service Response Time (Rank)	11(3)	8(1)	10(2)	12(4)
Disruption of Homes (Rank)	15(2)	14(1)	40(4)	20(3)
Disruption of Business (Rank)	2(1)	6(3)	10(4)	4(2)
Noise (Rank)	75(4)	65(2)	70(3)	50(1)
Users' Cost (Rank)	10(2)	10(2)	8(1)	12(3)

*Magnitude Ranks are in Brackets

To complete the matrix, we need 'importance weights to the impact area, which is given below (based on public surveys):

Market Access Time	4 in a scale of 1 to 10
Level of Service	5 in a scale of 1 to 10
Service Response Time	7 in a scale of 1 to 10
Disruption of Homes	10 in a scale of 1 to 10
Disruption of Businesses	10 in a scale of 1 to 10
Noise	6 in a scale of 1 to 10
Users' Cost	1 in a scale of 1 to 10

Following the standard practice of the matrix method, we have to compute the products of impact ranks and the 'importance' weights, i.e. $m_{ij} w_{ij}$ i= 1 to 7, j = 1 to 4. These are shown below in Table 3.4.

Table 3.4 Environmental Score for Highway Alternatives

Impact Areas (As Listed Above)	1	2	3	4
1	4×4=16	3×4=12	1×4=04	2×4=08
2	1×5=05	2×5=10	4×5=20	3×5=15
3	3×7=21	1×7=07	2×7=14	4×7=28
4	2×10=20	1×10=10	4×10=40	3×10=30
5	1×10=10	3×10=30	4×10=40	2×10=20
6	4×6=24	2×6=12	3×6=18	1×6=06
7	2×1=02	2×1=02	1×1=01	3×1=03
Total	98	83	137	110

Considering the nature of highway impacts, a lower impact score is better than a higher one. In this example, we have lowest total environmental score for highway alternative 2, so it is to be selected for implementation.

The matrix method of EIA as summarized above is quite comprehensive in coverage. Its interpretation and usefulness is well accepted. However, the predictive power of the method is weak.

Network Method

The network method of EIA basically uses the matrix approach by extending it further to take into account the primary as well as the secondary impacts in the cause action cumulative effects network framework. The network is shown in the form of a 'tree' which is also called as the 'relevance' or 'impact tree'. It may also be called a 'sequence diagram'. Identification of direct, indirect or short-term and long-term environmental impacts is a crucial and basic step of making the 'impact tree' or 'sequence diagram'. The conceptual framework for a linear network or impact tree is shown below in Fig. 3.1.

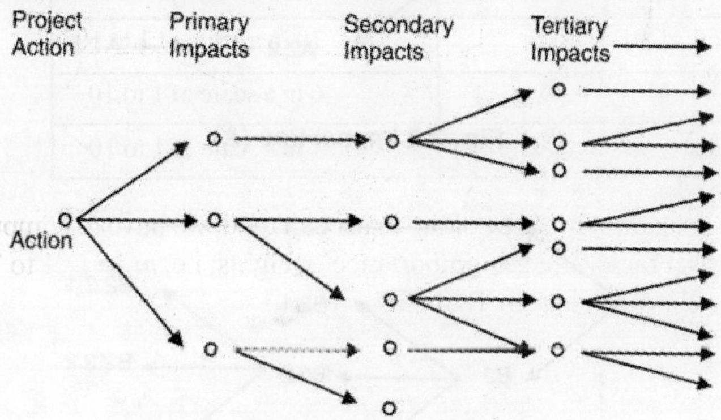

Fig. 3.1 A Conceptual network diagram

As Fig. 3.1 shows, a project action generates three primary impacts. These three primary impacts in sequence generate five secondary impacts and from these five impacts seven tertiary impacts are emerging. More than one action or primary impact may be a source of a secondary impact and so on.

The method is capable of providing us a summary index for assessing overall impacts of a project, though it will be a qualitative index in nature. The steps followed in construction of such an index are as follows:

1. Use the matrix method to assign ranks and importance weights to the estimated impacts on an impact-tree;
2. Estimate the occurrence probabilities of the individual chain of events on a branch of the impact-tree;
3. Sum-up the product of the probability that the event on the branch occur and the total impact score is obtained with the help of the matrix procedure.

Consider Fig. 3.2 and 3.3, A and B are two project activities. 'A' causes two primary impacts from which further impacts are caused as seen in the Figure. Similarly, 'B' causes two primary impacts from which secondary impacts are emerging and then tertiary impacts, as shown by the respective impact trees.

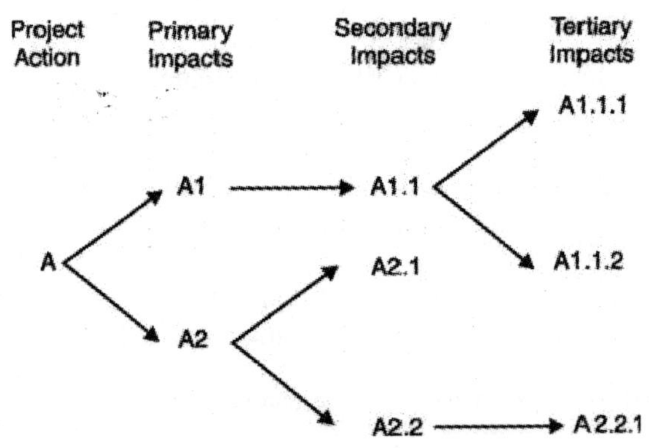

Fig. 3.2 Impact tree (A)

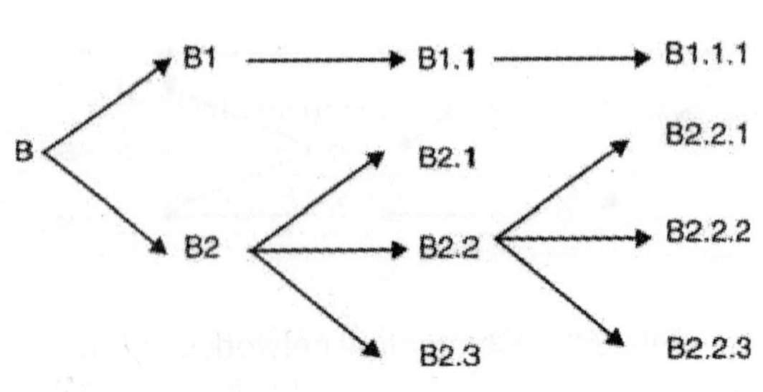

Fig. 3.3 Impact tree (B)

There are 10 impact branches in this figure, as follows:

(*a*) A1 $\rightarrow$ A1.1 $\rightarrow$ A1.1.1

(*b*) A1 $\rightarrow$ A1.1 $\rightarrow$ A1.1.2

(*c*) A2 $\rightarrow$ A2.1

(*d*) A2 $\rightarrow$ A2.2 $\rightarrow$ A2.2.1

(*e*) B1 $\rightarrow$ B1.1 $\rightarrow$ B1.1.1

(*f*) B2 $\rightarrow$ B2.1

(*g*) B2 $\rightarrow$ B2.2 $\rightarrow$ B2.2.1

(*h*) B2 $\rightarrow$ B2.2 $\rightarrow$ B2.2.2

(*i*) B2 $\rightarrow$ B2.2 $\rightarrow$ B2.2.3

(*j*) B2 $\rightarrow$ B2.3

Let p_i be the probability that the impacts on branch *i* occurs, $i = 1$ to 10 in this example

$M(X)$ = (+) or (–) magnitude of an impact X.

$I(X)$ = Importance weight for the impact X.

The impact-score for any impact-tree branch would be $\Sigma M(X) I(X)$ where summation is over all impacts X on the branch.

For example, for the above branches we have:

1. M(A1) I(A1) + M(A1.1) I(A1.1) + M(A1.1.1) I(A1.1.1)
2. M(A1) I(A1) + M(A1.1) I(A1.1) + M(A1.1.2) I(A1.1.2)
3. M(A2) I(A2) + M(A2.1) I(A2.1)
4. M(A2) I(A2) + M(A2.2) I(A2.2) + M(A2.2.1) I(A2.2.1)

Similarly, we express the impact-scores for the branches related to the action B.

$$\text{Expected environmental impact score} = \sum_{1}^{10} p_i \text{ (Impact score for Branch } i)$$

$i = 1$ to 10 (in this example).

Let us consider a branch of impact 'tree' for a highway project as:

The probabilities for these four impacts are given as 1.0, 1.0, 1.0, 0.1 respectively. The magnitudes and 'importance' weights in ranks are also given as shown in the following calculation.

Branch Impact Score = (–4) (5) + (–3) (6) + (–1) (7) + (–1) (1) = –46

The probability for occurrence of the impacts on the branch would be (1.0) (1.0) (1.0) (0.1) = 0.1. The probability weighted branch impact score, i.e. the expected impact-score would be (0.1) (–46) = –4.6.

Similar calculations would be made for other impact branches related to all actions of the project. The sum of all such probability weighted branch impact scores would give us the 'total expected' branch impact-score for the project as a whole.

The network method is useful in the sense that it covers the anticipated cumulative environmental impacts in the EIA cause-condition-effect framework. Its success depends on meaningful estimation of the chances, i.e. probabilities of occurrence of individual impacts. The estimation of magnitudes of the impacts is also equally important for their ranking. 'Impact-trees' of the method are very much convenient for communication of information to interested groups or public at large.

3.3 AIR QUALITY IMPACT ASSESSMENT

3.3.1 Planning of Air Impact Assessment Exercise

This is a general description of planning and management of impact studies, applicable to all aspects of environment and not only to air pollution assessment. This kind of exercise includes:

1. A conceptual approach for planning and conducting environmental impact study;
2. Proposal for new development project or plan or action;
3. Interdisciplinary team formation for conducting impact study;
4. Selection of team leader;
5. General study management;
6. Fiscal control.

All these steps are self-explanatory. Only some more clarification is required regarding the conceptual study as the impact assessment procedure or methodology will be based on it.

According to Westman (1985), an impact assessment exercise runs in terms of seven phases. The first phase is concerned with defining the study goals. It is a pre-impact assessment exercise, mainly a table-work related to a brief description of the project, its location and other such details. The second phase is concerned with identification of potential impacts. It is what we call as 'scooping' step of the EIA. The third phase is crucial. It is concerned with measuring baseline conditions of environment in the project area, prediction of environmental impacts of the proposed project/action and summarizing and analyzing the findings. In the fourth phase, the significant impacts are evaluated. This may lead to modifications of proposed actions, determination of alternative actions, and mitigation measures. All this is done in the fifth phase. The sixth phase is to communicate findings and recommendations to the decision-makers and to take the decision about the project/action. The final phase is concerned to monitor effects of actions and further modification of mitigation measures.

3.3.2 Assessment of Impacts

To assess environmental impacts, in general, we need a methodology. This is derived from the planning phases of the impact studies. Once a decision for conducting a comprehensive EIA study related to a project/or action is taken, we actually start it from the third phase of the planning. It involves:

1. Identification of baseline or existing environmental conditions in the area of the proposed project;
2. A description or prediction of future changes in the environmental conditions without the project;
3. Prediction of environmental impacts associated with the project during its construction periods;
4. Mitigating procedures for the adverse impacts and suggestion of alternatives;
5. Communication of study results to the decision-makers.

For air pollution impact analysis, we follow this approach starting with the assessment of the baseline conditions concerning air pollution and climate in the project affected area.

Baseline Environmental Assessment

Knowledge of the existing air quality conditions prevailing in the area is essential irrespective of the planned development of the project. This helps us in assessing the project specific air pollution levels in the area concerned. For baseline study of air pollution, we need to obtain measurements of the ambient levels of the pollutants of concern at one or more locations in the study area. Keeping in mind the guidelines of the government agencies responsible for environmental protection, we need information regarding:

(*a*) types and concentration of hazardous gaseous chemical emissions and their environmental effects;

(*b*) particulate matters;

(*c*) offensive odors; and

(*d*) various climatic conditions.

The land-use patterns like agriculture, industries, residential complexes, commercial activities, play-grounds, vehicular traffic, etc. all air polluting sources may be examined carefully for their contribution in generating air pollution in the concerned area and around it. 'Regional air quality', 'sub-regional air quality' and 'local air quality' are to be assessed by using the secondary data available from the various sources. Sometimes, for some information, one may need field surveys and measurement of ambient air pollution. This may be done with the help of the pollution measuring instruments. Air pollution is greatly affected by the meteorological conditions prevailing in a region.

It is desirable to build an 'emission inventory' for major air pollutants if it is not readily available for the place or region under consideration. An 'emission inventory' provides a summary of the air pollutant emission under current conditions in the vicinity of the proposed project activity. The steps associated with making an emission inventory are as follows:

(*i*) Classification of air pollutants and the sources of their emissions in the geographical area under consideration.

(*ii*) Identification and aggregation of information on emissions factors for each of the identified pollutants and sources. An 'emission factor' is the average rate at which a pollutant is released into the atmosphere as a result of some activity such as combustion of industrial pollution. The 'emission factors' relate to the types and quantities of pollutants emitted to indicators like production capacity, quantity of fuel burned or vehicle-miles travelled by an automobile; such as particulates per ton of coal burned.

(*iii*) Determination of the daily quantity of material handled, processed or burned or other unit production information.

(*iv*) Computation of the rate at which each type of pollutant is released to the atmosphere.

(*v*) Summation of the specific pollutant emissions from each of the identified source categories.

Through the information available from the existing emission inventory in the project region, it may be compared with the ambient air-quality standards to access the state of air pollution prior to the initiation of the developmental projects.

Having established the baseline pollution levels, it is then necessary to consider how these levels are expected to change in the future irrespective of the possible effects of the proposed project. If the emissions sources and strength and the climatic conditions in the area are not expected to change in future then the current baseline air quality would represent the future baseline air quality. But this is unlikely as population and land use pattern of the area may change over time, new developmental projects may come up, fuel substitution might take place, number of vehicles on roads may go up and to some extent climatic conditions might change. The process of predicting future baseline conditioning will be similar to the method of predicting pollution consequences of the proposed new project.

Identification of Project Related Pollutant Emissions and Assessing their Impacts

The types of pollutants generated during the construction period and later on during its operational phase should be analyzed separately. The basic purpose of the analysis is to see how the baseline ambient air quality prevailing in the project location and around it would change as a result of implementing the project. This is done by comparing the projected baseline air quality without the project with future ambient air quality with the project.

Impact Prediction

This exercise is basically devoted to assess the impacts of new projects on ambient air quality. Most popular ones are (*i*) the mass-balance approach, and (*ii*) use of mathematical models.

(*i*) **Mass-Balance Approach:** Under such approaches, we may consider air pollutant emissions from the construction and operational phases of the project activity in relation to the existing 'emission-inventory' of the study area. An 'emission-inventory' representing a mass balance of the total air pollutant emissions from all sources for a proposed project or activity entering the atmosphere during the construction and/or operational phases should be prepared. Once such an inventory is prepared, the next step is to have a 'mesoscale impact calculation'. This is, simply, to find the increase in the existing (baseline) emission inventory for one or more air pollutants as a result of the project activities. Mathematical relation used for this purpose is:

Percentage increase in Inventory =

$$100 \times \frac{\text{Emission Inventory Information with Project}}{\text{Existing Inventory Information}}$$

Such increases (in index form) can be calculated for each pertinent pollutant and each phase of the project activity (construction and operation). A total percentage increase could be calculated by summing the values of all pollutants in the inventory. The indices for individual pollutants as well for their total can be interpreted keeping in mind the standards.

(*ii*) **Mathematical Models:** A number of mathematical models have been developed to predict air pollutant dispersions and concentrations. The most popular mathematical models are: (*i*) Box Model, (*ii*) Dispersion or Gaussian Models and (*iii*) Computer Simulation Model. 'Box Model' is a simple mathematical approach used to calculate ground-level concentration of specific air pollutants emitted from the project activity. Model is based on the assumption that pollutants emitted to the atmosphere are uniformly mixed in a volume or 'box' of air. Dimensions of the 'box' represent with rationale the down wind, cross wind and vertical inversions. The time period for mixing the pollutant in the box is normally assumed to be one hour and during the period of pollutant mixing the steady state conditions prevail in the atmosphere. Further it is assumed that the pollutants mix completely and instantaneously with the air, and the released material is chemically stable. Mathematical expression of the 'box model' is :

$$C = \frac{Q \cdot T}{X \cdot Y \cdot Z}$$

where

C = average concentration of gas or particulate < 20 mg in size in $\mu g/m^{3.}$

Q = release rate of gas or particulate pollutant from the source(s) μg/sec, related to emission factor information.

T = time period over which pollutant mixing is done uniformly in the 'box' usually 1 hour.

X = downward dimension of the box in meters based on average wind speed and physical aspect of terrain represented by the box.

Y = cross-wind dimension of box, m, (based on average wind-speed, source configuration, and physical aspect of the terrain).

Z = vertical dimension of the box, m, (based on limiting inversion heights in the area and physical terrain).

The box model can be used for single point source, multiple point sources, area, line or mixed type of sources of air pollutants. There are several air-quality dispersion models. They are classified into a variety of ways like; according to source type, pollutant type, time basis (long-term and short-term) and atmospheric reaction type (smog formation, acid rains, deposition, etc). Some of the models are simple manual calculator base while others are computer based. Recent trend is, of course, of using computers with readymade software programmes.

In short, we can say that models can be useful in estimating the impacts of the project activities on air quality. Selection of an appropriate model for prediction of air pollution levels depends on technical consideration such as assumptions of the model, data requirements and skills required to handle it.

There are some special considerations related to pollutant emissions from nuclear establishments, fossil-fueled power plants and industrial plants due to accidental releases. A risk or safety analysis of such releases must be incorporated in the normal air quality impact assessment exercise.

Assessing Impact Significance

The potentially significant impacts related to a project or action will be addressed at the stage of 'scooping'. The completion of the impact prediction exercise for the project would provide quantitative magnitudes or indices for them. In the context of air quality impact analysis and such magnitude may be evaluated carefully. Professional judgment would be quite helpful in this regard.

Mitigation Measures

Mitigation measures are the activities that are to be adopted to reduce the air quality degradation associated with the proposed project. A major step of the mitigation process is to revise the design of the project to reduce the expected air pollutants released by its activities. However, it may not be possible to eliminate the air pollution completely as technological alternatives for revision of the project may be limited or too costly. Some general mitigation measures would have to be adopted depending on the nature of the project, its scale, location, etc. A few mitigation measures as suggested by various authors are as follows:

1. Restriction on practices of open burning the agricultural crop residues and dry leaves.
2. Open land becomes a major source of particulate air pollution because of wind erosion of soil. This can be checked temporarily by watering the land. Some alternatives for watering of open land are: (*i*) Use of chemicals to stabilize dust on open surfaces; (*ii*) Construction of wind breaker. This is also costly and less effective; (*iii*) Having vegetation cover of the area by planting fast growing grasses, bushes and trees.
3. Unpaved roads must be watered or paved or chemically treated.

4. Fugitive-dust control measures for open-waste piles and staging areas; dry surface impoundments; land-falls, land treatment systems, and waste stabilization measures, etc. can be adopted to minimize air pollution.
5. Control on pesticide uses in order to reduce emission of liquid pesticide particulate emission in the air.
6. Strict control of automobile vehicle emissions as per the national standards and regulations is the most important mitigation measure of air pollution control in urban areas. It may be supplemented with the use of alternative eco-friendly fuel, like methanol in vehicles. Traffic planning and land-use patterns, must be linked with air pollution reduction. Provisions for mass transit, car pool systems, bicycle lanes, etc.
7. The use of exhaust emission control technologies for mobile and stationary air pollution sources must be encouraged wherever it is plausible.

   In short, we can say that (*a*) application of control technology to further reduce air-pollution attributed to the projects; (*b*) burning operations during periods of favorable meteorological conditions; (*c*) reduction in vehicle uses by providing alternative transit routes; (*d*) reduction of emissions from all sources in the vicinity of the project including it, and the residential areas; (*e*) provision of green belts around cities and greater emphasis on vegetation growing to control air pollution, are some important considerations for air pollution control. The success of all mitigation measures of course, depends on effective management and implementation strategies of the measures.

3.4 NOISE IMPACT ANALYSIS

3.4.1 Environmental Impacts of Noise

A noise problem from man's point of view exists when it interferes with his activities. Some specific human activities that are affected by loud noise are as follows:

1. Damage to hearing and health.
2. Interference with work tasks.
3. Interference with speech communication.
4. Effects on inter-room privacy.
5. Interference with sleep.
6. Annoyance or irritation.

A man having hearing deficiency is treated as physically handicapped. Most of the human communication is through speech and hearing. Hearing is very important for human development with improved quality of life.

Loud sounds damage human (or animal) ear which is a very sensitive and versatile organ. Although human beings are capable of hearing sounds upto 140 dBA without any pain but continuous exposure to noise pollution in the range of 100 to 140 dBA or more of it will damage the ear permanently. Even an impulsive sound of very high intensity will make him deaf forever. The ideal noise free environment is considered to be upto 50 dBA depending upon the types of activities.

Hearing loss due to continuous exposure to loud noise is seen in practice by a gradual shift of the hearing threshold. It has been demonstrated that the length of exposure is as important as the magnitude of the noise in producing hearing loss. Continuous exposure to loud noise produces disruption and damages to the nerve cells of the organ. This is a series effect of noise on human life. In order to protect those people who are continuously exposed to high noise levels, particularly for industrial workers, exposure limits are fixed by the law in most of the developed and leading developing countries of the world.

Some Indian limits, very much similar to OSHA (Occupational Safety and Health Administration of USA) limits are as follows:

Table 3.5 Damage Risk Criteria for Hearing Loss

Noise Level dBA Slow Response	Maximum Time of Exposure (hours)
90	8
92	6
95	4
97	3
100	2
105	1
110	0.5
115	0.25 or less

The noise exposure levels (hours and dBA) for non-occupational noise situations are rarely specified. The Environmental Protection Agency (EPA) of USA, however, recommends 85 dBA as the noise exposure limit for public which if exceeded may cause hearing damages. This limit is considerably low (75 dBA) in the case of occupational workers.

Person to person conversation, class-room lecturing and listening to television and radio, etc. are all affected adversely by the background noise.

The interference of noise with verbal communication is called 'masking'. The degree of masking of speech depends on variety of factors. The overall degree of 'masking' is measured in terms of the percentage of spoken messages or phrases understood by the listener. Experiments have shown that relaxed conversation is virtually impossible when the ambient noise level is 70 dBA or more. Even with a raised voice, satisfactory communication to a person located at least 1.5 metres from the speaker is not easy with such a level of noise pollution. The safe limit of out-door noise for noise free speech is only 55 dBA or less.

The interference of noise with sleep is a widely observed fact. A person may have deep sleep or no sleep or light or disturbed sleep due to noise. The effect of noise on sleep thus depends on factors like motivation to wake, loudness and duration of the noise, fluctuations of noise, sleep deprivation, physiological difference between men and women, age differences, familiarity with noise, etc.

Awakening from a light stage of sleep is caused by noise levels as low as 30 to 40 dBA. The percentage of awakening time increases to 90 when sound level is 80 dBA. A daily average level of 45 dBA sound should be sufficient to protect majority of population from the adverse health effects of sleep loss due to noise.

There are other effects of noise such as on performance of tasks, adverse psychological and physiological effects, mental illness, blood circulatory problems, heart diseases, etc.

The effect of noise on domestic and wild animals is quite well known to us. Similarly, property values like housing prices are adversely affected due to noise pollution. Strong protective measures are undertaken by the states all over the world to protect people from the adverse effects of noise pollution. This includes noise regulatory guidelines and ambient standards for compliance.

There is no separate law or Act for noise pollution control in India. It is included under the Air (Prevention and Control) Act of 1981. Following the provisions of the Act, the Central Pollution Control Board (CPCB) has developed the following standards for noise levels in the air (given in Table 3.6).

Table 3.6 CPCB Standards for Noise Pollution Control in India

Area Code	Category of Area	Limits in Day time*	dBA Night Time*
A	Industrial Area	75	70
B	Commercial Area	65	55
C	Residential Area	55	45
D**	Silence Zone	50	40

* Day Time: 6 a.m. to 9 p.m.

* Night Time: 9 p.m. to 6 a.m.

** Silence Zone covers the area around 100 metres from the hospital, educational institutions and courts. Use of vehicular horns, loudspeakers and bursting of crackers shall be banned in these areas.

The WHO's (World Health Organization) safe limit of noise pollution is only 45 dB.

3.4.2 Noise Impact Assessment

The general methodology for assessing noise impacts has the following steps:

1. General description of the project, its site plan and assessing the existing baseline noise environment;
2. Project characteristics, its noise potential and ambient noise standards;
3. Prediction of noise impacts;
4. Determination of significant impacts;
5. Mitigation measures including alternatives.

Assessment of Baseline Noise Environment

This step is necessary in order to predict or to assess the noise impacts of the project. Basically noise impacts are local in type so there will be no problem of delineation of study area for assessing the baseline noise environment.

The baseline study of noise environment requires data on (*a*) the noise levels and (*b*) noise sources. Such data may be collected either from the various published sources or through a primary survey. This provides information concerning all source emissions of noise, their location, magnitude of noise, frequency duration and relative contribution of the sources in noise emissions. Sources are normally categorized as residential activities, manufacturing activities, transportation, trade, services and cultural-cum-entertainment and recreational activities. Factories, markets, schools, playgrounds, transportation modes and airports, military training centers, etc. are all major noise sources.

In the context of baseline noise assessment, one can measure total ambient noise levels at different and carefully selected noise locations through appropriate noise meters. Timings of measurement may be on hourly basis, peak noise hour or whatever is the requirement of the regulatory law. Noise is primarily a local impact. Noise contours depicting the impacted areas will clearly reflect this. It will be at higher levels in urban industrial and commercial areas, and urban residential areas. The sub-urban areas and even rural areas will also be quite noise sometimes. All such variations should be taken into account in the baseline impact analysis.

An important aspect of the baseline noise impact assessment is to find the impact of noise on peoples' health, communication, and other aspects of human life. How wildlife is being affected by it should also be assessed. The percentage of people feeling annoyance due to noise level is a very important aspect of noise pollution.

Once the baseline noise assessment is made, the next step would be to predict the future noise scenario in the project area without the proposed project. Noise generating sources like population, industrial and commercial growth, and other activities in a region are expected to change in future. How such changes would affect the future noise environment is necessary to be known in order to assess the project specific changes in the noise levels. The methods for the baseline noise prediction are similar to that of the noise prediction for the new project.

Project Characteristics and Its Noise Potential

Given the baseline noise environment, the next step of noise impact assessment is to see how this will be changing in future with implementation of the proposed project. For this, we have to describe first the noise potential of the project during its construction period and later on when it is fully operational. For all this, a future noise inventory will be made through prediction of all project associated noise level.

Noise Prediction

The basic purpose of this step is to identify the noise levels which may occur both in short-term and long-term as a result of the development resulting from the accumulation of background noise sources. The whole exercise of noise prediction is very much complex. The list of noise dimensions or variables for example, may be as follows..

(*a*) Prediction of baseline noise environmental changes in future.

(*b*) The type of equipment, both the fixed and mobile, to be used at the proposed project.

(*c*) The duration of various levels of construction and operation and the total time span for prediction of noise.

(*d*) The time of day when the equipment is to be used.

(*e*) The attitude of site operator.

(*f*) The location of receivers and their classification, e.g. residences, schools, hospitals, markets, etc.

(*g*) The topography of area including the land-use patterns and natural noise barriers.

(*h*) Meteorological conditions in the area.

The type of equipment to be used in construction and the operational plant and equipment of the project are the technical considerations.

Apart from the equipments there will be several other project construction activities which make noise. They are to be taken into consideration for noise forecasting.

If a sound is created at a point such as a generator, a system of spherical waves propagates through the air at a speed of 1100 feet per second. As the wave propagates, its height or the intensity diminishes. This phenomenon is called 'attenuation of sound'. A point source of sound such as construction equipment or a thermal power house or a factory uses this principle of sound wave propagation from the source. A simple mathematical model used in noise forecasting is as follows:

$$L_2 = L_1 - 10 \log \left(\frac{r_2}{r_1}\right)^2$$

where L_1 is the sound pressure level at location 1 at a distance r_1 and L_2 is the sound pressure level at the distance r_2. This is called as the 'inverse square law', r_1 and r_2 are, in fact, the radii of the sound concentric waves around the point source. For every doubling of distance in this formula sound pressure decreases by 6 dBA. If there are physical barriers to sound propagation, atmospheric absorptions of sound and climatic influences, then the sound levels can be reduced further.

The line sources propagate sound emissions under movement. The above formula for estimating sound level L_2 at a distance r_2 if sound level at a distance r_1 is known, is modified as:

$$L_2 = L_1 - 10 \log \left(\frac{r_2}{r_1}\right)$$

For each doubling of the distance from a line source the sound level will decrease by only 3 dBA.

Simple mathematical models for noise prediction have been developed for specific sources like highways, airports, military installations and construction operations. Such models take into account impulsive sound and/or continuous sound waves. Apart from this, there are several; comprehensive mathematical models with provision of software packages to predict noise levels from different projects. Sometimes noise experience of similar projects elsewhere may provide good background matcrial for noise forecasting. This may be explored by comparing the land use patterns around the two project areas.

Environmental noise may also be predicted through statistical technique of regression analysis. Suppose, we consider a city. The city is noisy because of too many people living in it (P), existence of industries (I), traffic in the city (T) and so on. We may specify a relationship like N = f(P,I,T,....), where N is the noise level in dBA. By taking time-series or cross-sectional data of the variables concerning noisy locations or cities, the regression equation can be fitted which will provide a base for predicting future noise levels. This approach is good for predicting ambient noise levels with and without the project, provided the project effects are captured by the independent variables of the equation.

Assessment of Impact Significance

Once the information regarding the baseline noise environment, its future pattern, i.e. the future noise environment without the project, and the future noise environment with the project is available, the project specific noise levels can be assessed by taking their differences. The increase in noise levels should also be compared with the national standards for determining their significance. If a change in noise levels with and without the project or development is 3 dBA, it is barely detectable, a change of 5 dBA is clearly detectable, and a change of 10 dBA linked with doubling of the noise levels. There may be variations in defining severity of noise impacts depending on national ambient noise levels. As mentioned earlier, noise pollution impacts are more or less highly localized depending on the land use patterns. An increase in noise in an area which is already having high ambient noise levels may be more significant than a similar increase in an area with lower noise levels.

The same level of noise at a noise sensitive area (schools, hospitals, courts, etc.) will be most significant than at a less sensitive area.

Mitigation Measures and Monitoring

Whenever ambient noise levels exceed the tolerance limits, we need to reduce them in order to protect the human beings and wildlife from adverse impacts. The problem of noise control has three elements: production of noise at the source(s), propagation of noise in the atmosphere, and receiving of the noise by the receivers: human being and wildlife. Noise can be controlled at the source and/or its propagation may be obstructed in order to have smaller noise levels at the receiver end and/or the receiver may be shifted farther away to have less impact of the noise.

Control of noise at the source can be effective in a variety of ways. The equipment used or the mode of operation can be changed to produce less noise. The sources of noise may be enclosed with sound proof material or vibration reducing or sound absorbing material and if, possible, be shifted away from the receivers provided it is technically and economically feasible. Further, the timing of the noise making source operations must be regulated.

Aircrafts, transport vehicles, military exercises are branded as noise makers. Their operations must be regulated strictly according to the noise control guidelines.

Noise propagation through air must be controlled by putting noise barriers on its way so that there is maximum possible noise leakage during its transmission stage and the receivers get less of it. Noise enclosures, and noise barriers are technically quite sound.

Noise screens can consist of topographical features or tree plantings as well as artificial materials. Earth mounds or bunds are often built alongside roads to absorb and deflect traffic noise away from the nearby residential areas and other buildings. Planting of dense trees and under-bushes provide a natural barrier to traffic noise propagation on highways. Thick areas of dense trees and bushes may reduce noise by 3 to 4 dBA at low frequencies and 10 to 12 dBA at higher frequencies. A new method of noise control is, to build 'green wall'. It is a wall of woven dormant willow shoots 2 metres apart which are filled with soil and an in-built watering system.

Artificial materials are used as sound barriers. Some widely used materials are: concrete blocks and walls 4 to 6 inches thick (noise reduction 36 to 40 dBA); granite blocks 4 to 6 inches (40 dBA); bricks 4 inches (33 dBA): glass 1/4 inch (26 dBA); wood: Fir 2 inches and pine 2 inches (24, 22 dBA), Aluminium 1/4 inch (27 dBA), steel 20 ga (22 dBA), plywood 2 inches (22 dBA), Lead 1/16 inch (8 dBA).

Noise control at the receiver end is almost similar to that as at the source end. Proper site planning may protect people from the project noise pollution. Houses and sensitive activities like schools, hospitals, should be located away from the noise affected zones. Housing design should be such that its walls automatically act as noise barriers. Noise screens can be erected to protect receivers from highway and other types of noise emissions.

Several other measures include traffic controls, proper maintenance or roads within the cities, ban on loudspeakers, shifting of noise making fixed sources away from the densely populated areas, proper city planning, proper regulation of outdoor sports activities, music festivals, etc. There is a strong need of changing the attitude of noise makers through educating them at least informally about the adverse effects of noise on human beings and wildlife. A noise free environment is as essential for good life as drinking of clean water and breathing in pure, pollutant free air. Monitoring of noise control is as essential as the mitigation measures for this. The primary responsibility of this lies with the project management and government agencies.

3.5 WATER QUALITY IMPACT ANALYSIS

3.5.1 Water Impact Factors

Number of factors related to project actions, plans, programmes, and policies affect water quantity and quality directly and indirectly. Some of the crucial factors linked with water related impacts can be listed as follows:

1. Growth of population in several countries leads to the increase in demand for water in relation to its supply.
2. Living styles of people, their ignorance related to water quality damages by their own actions.
3. Lack of adequate and unscientific management of water resources.
4. Urban and suburban growth leads to increase in demand for water for various purposes and affects its quality parameters.
5. Industrial expansion leads to increase in water demand, waste waters from various activities lead to a damage to surface as well as ground water quality.
6. Power plants' requirements of water for cooling towers and release of the waste water spoils water quality and the aquatic life.
7. Municipal waste water treatment plants discharge primary, secondary and tertiary treated waste waters on grounds and streams.
8. Dredging projects in rivers, harbors, estuaries, and/on coastal area leading to increase in turbidity and release of sediment contaminants in water.
9. Projects involving 'fill' or creation of 'fast lands' along rivers, lakes, estuaries and coastal areas.
10. Highway projects particularly in hilly areas.
11. Construction of dams for the purpose of water supply, flood control and hydroelectricity generation.
12. River channelization projects for flow improvements.
13. Mining projects.
14. Agricultural/irrigation practices.
15. Forest management practices and deforestation.
16. Commercial hazardous waste disposal sites.
17. Tourism projects adjoining to estuaries and coastal areas.

How some of the above listed factors affect the water quality and quantity can be seen from Table 3.7 in which a checklist of 11 projects or activities and 26 water quality indicators are shown.

Table 3.7 Potential Impacts from Major Projects

Environmental Indicators	Impacts of Projects or Activity										
	1	2	3	4	5	6	7	8	9	10	11
Surface Stream Discharge		*	*			*		*		*	
Surface Water Quality (Temperature)	*			*	*	*		*		*	*
BOD			*	*			*			*	
Dissolved Oxygen			*	*	*	*					
Suspended Solids	*	*	*	*			*	*	*	*	*
Turbidity	*	*	*	*			*	*	*	*	*
Total Dissolved Solids		*	*	*	*				*	*	
pH				*		*			*		
Bacteria and Viruses			*	*		*					
Nitrogen			*	*	*	*	*	*		*	*
Phosphorous		*	*	*		*		*		*	
Hardness				*					*	*	
Iron and Manganese				*		*	*				
Chlorides		*	*	*						*	
Heavy Metals				*	*		*		*		
Radioactivity				*	*				*		
Pesticides				*			*			*	*
Toxic Substances				*							
Stratification					*	*					
Flooding			*			*		*			
Ground Water Quantity		*	*							*	
Water Quality			*							*	
Erosion	*	*	*			*		*	*	*	*
Sedimentation	*	*	*			*	*	*	*	*	*
Water Demand			*	*	*				*	*	
Waste Water System			*	*	*					*	
Indicators Affected	5	9	17	19	9	12	8	9	10	17	7

Columns

(1) Construction

(2) Highway

(3) Urban/Sub-urban Growth

(4) Industrial Expansion

(5) Power Plants

(6) Dams and Reservoirs

(7) Dredging

(8) Channelisation

(9) Mining

(10) Agriculture/Irrigation

(11) Forest Management

Construction activities are usually temporary, lasting only upto the construction period. Soil erosion from the construction site, increased sedimentation downstream from the construction site, increased suspended solids in water nearby the site, and consequently the effect of turbidity of water are a few water quality impacts of construction. Surface and groundwater may be affected by these but the impacts will be significant for small and local streams.

Highways are important land use patterns. Surface stream discharges, suspended solids in water, turbidity, total dissolved solids, possibility of increased phosphorous concentration and silica in the nearby streams are other water quality impacts of highways during the construction period. After construction, elements in automobile exhausts are released into the atmosphere and a part of that may find their ways into local water courses. Spills from trucks carrying chemicals and petroleum products may pollute water systems near highways. Highways may also be linked with flooding through breaches in their embankments.

Urban/sub-urban growth results in increased demand for water. This places additional stress on existing water supply sources, water treatment systems, water distributing system, and waste water flows. Dust and chemicals deposited on the land surface will be carried on the storm water into the run-offs. Increased urbanization and associated industrial and commercials activities result in more rapid accumulation of various pollutants on the Earth's surface which eventually affect the surface and groundwater. Increased soil erosion is also linked with urbanization because of several developmental activities like roads, buildings, airports, railway station, parks, etc.

Industries are regarded as the top water polluters. The industrial waste water containing several dangerous contaminants finally reach to the nearby water stream and ground, polluting the water and making it quite unfit. All kinds of contaminants, biological, physical, chemical, and even radiological, are emitted by the industries and it is quite cheap for them to dispose off all that in the rivers as there is no effective control over them for not doing so. Treatment of industrial waste before throwing it into river water and recycling of the treated water are the only mitigation measures for controlling river water pollution by the industries.

Power plants are polluting water in the same way as the other industries. They release hot waste water from their cooling towers and other processes affecting the aquatic life adversely or destroying it all together. Nuclear plants may be cited as "the killer" of the biotic life.

Blocking of flowing water in rivers by constructing dams and reservoirs has been regarded as a water quality damaging activity. Losses of terrestrial habitats, agricultural lands, buildings, rise of local water tables, local climatic changes, fog, water bound pathogens, earthquakes, loss of forests, etc. are a few major adverse impacts of dams and reservoirs on biota. The downstream water quantity and quality are severely affected by these. Decreased dispersion of waste discharges along the shorelines, reduced re-aeration caused by the depths and reduced velocities, changes in water tastes, odors resulting in from algal activities, accumulation of sludge and thermal stratification of waste, are other adverse impacts on aquatic environment because of impounding of water in large reservoirs. Positive impacts are availability of water goes up, turbidity is reduced, hardness of water decreases, BOD reduces and coliform density reduces.

Agricultural operations do cause several direct and indirect impacts on water quality. There is stream sedimentation increase in nutrients, pesticides and salt concentration in run offs. Animal waste is another water polluting material coming from the agricultural activities. As Table 3.7 shows, 17 water quality variables are affected by agriculture and irrigation activities making it a major water polluter at par with industries and urban growth.

Destruction of forests because of land pressure and their exploitation on increasing rates for economic benefits like wood are causing concern for depleting water sources over land surface as well as underground. Forest management activities like logging, clear cutting are encouraging soil erosion and thus, increased turbidity in receiving water streams. Table 3.7 shows, 7 water quality indicators are affected by the forest management activity.

Water quality impacts of other activities like dredging, channelization and mining operations are also there.

3.5.2 Water Quality Impact Analysis

We may list the steps as following:

1. Identification of the types of water quantity and quality impacts related to the project/action which are to be assessed and a brief introduction of the project/action. This step is basically what we call as the 'scooping' step.
2. Baseline environmental setting concerning the hydrological environment and assessment of existing water quantity and quality impacts in the light of prevailing standards.
3. Prediction of the water quantity and quality impacts for future (i.e. without the project).
4. Prediction of water impacts with the project.
5. Identification of project related significant impacts.
6. Mitigation measures for maintaining water quantity and quality standards including alternatives to the project.

Identification of Impacts for Assessment and Project Introduction

This step of EIA is devoted to summarize the features of the proposed project. And the likely water impacts associated with it. The basic issues to be focused are:

1. The type of project and how it functions in technical sense;
2. The impact area and potential water impacts associated with it;
3. The parameters that should be included in the study and the level of accuracy for them;
4. Availability of secondary data related to hydrology;
5. Data to be collected through field surveys;
6. The possible mitigation measures and need for monitoring of the water quality in the region, and
7. The possible alternatives that could be considered for the project.

This will be basically a desk job to collect all the above mentioned information with minimum field surveys.

Water quality impact assessor is having the services of the interdisciplinary team having the specialists of hydrology in it. All issues of EIA are to be considered. Most important of them is the selection of appropriate hydrological and water quality indicators for the study. Existing water quantity and quality environment in the project area is assessed based on it.

Assessment of Baseline Water Quality and Quantity

This step of water quality impact assessment focuses on the physical parameters related to the aquatic environment and the water quality indicators. Following aspects concerning to study area is studied:

1. Topography	Relief Size: catchment size and character Drainage areas Flood Plain, extent, nature and current uses
2. Geology and Soils	Types, characteristics and depth
3. Rainfall and frequency	Seasonal, annual, storm frequency, and drought Short term variations in these parameters in the Project catchment area, and weather station patterns Interception
4. Snow	Seasonal, annual and extreme levels
5. Dew and Fog	Seasonal
6. Evaporation	Actual evapo-transpiration—seasonal and annual
7. Infiltration	Average and extreme values
8. Soil Water	Soil moisture levels- short-term, seasonal, annual and long-term
9. Ground Water	Aquifers- location, porosity, permeability and yield Recharge/discharge areas and rates, flow rates Water table levels/storage, short-term, long-term, seasonal, annual Patterns of flows
10. Standing Water (Ponds, Lakes, etc.)	Location and elevation, dimensions and capacity
11. Runoff	Inter flow, overland flow-frequency and magnitude Channel flow, seasonal, annual, long-term and extreme
12. Flood risk	Flood frequency and magnitude Flood control facilities
13. Erosion and Sedimentation	Soil erodability and location of erosion Channel erosion and location problem Stream load and location of sedimentation
14. Drainage	Effect on wetlands and location problems
15. Water Use	Total, drinking, agricultural, urban, industrial (seasonal, annual) Abstraction sources (rivers, reservoirs and ground water) Water importation/diversion
16. Water Budget	Components of the budget equation

Water quality indicators are to be considered for assessing the baseline aquatic environment. It will be studied for all water systems: rivers, lakes, ponds, ground water, and soil water from the perspective of human health, fisheries, and other aquatic life.

For hydrological data, the concerned departments like Geological Survey of India, Irrigation Department, Meteorological Stations, Irrigation Research Institutes, Central Water and Power Commission in India, and Universities may be a good source. A field survey process may also be initiated to fill up the data gaps and assess the water scenario in the study area.

Chemical methods are used for analyzing water samples for relevant determinants of water quality like concentration of nitrates and other toxic materials, BOD, COD, and physical properties like pH, radioactivity, etc. Such methods normally give accurate estimations of the contaminants. Some pollutants like micro-organic compounds present in water are both, difficult and expensive to monitor. The biotic methods use plants or animals as indirect ways of measuring water quality. Several groups of freshwater organisms have been used as indicators of given water pollution problems, the most common of them is the use of macro-invertebrate families for detecting water pollution levels as they can survive in water with low levels of dissolved oxygen. Changes in fish populations with time can give information about long-term pollution trends such as acidification and eutrophication. Higher plants are also used as indicators of water and sediment quality.

Pathogens in water can be detected either individually as species/strains or as indicator groups/species. The most common indicator organisms used are coliform bacteria both natural and fecal.

Existing or baseline water environment should be aimed at making of an inventory of water sources with respect to both quantity and quality for the project area. This will be used as a base for assessing the project related future water impacts in the area. The water quality standards for various uses and effluent discharges, etc. must be taken into account to assess baseline water quality.

Prediction of Changes in Baseline Water Environment

This step is concerned with the prediction of changes in the baseline water environment in future without the project. It arises from (*i*) climatic changes, (*ii*) natural changes, and (*iii*) impacts of future developmental changes on water quality in the area. These elements are not very easy to be predicted precisely. On the basis of the past observations, they may be predicted. The approaches for water impact prediction as summarized in the next sub-section can also be used for prediction of the baseline changes.

Prediction of Water Impacts Associated with a Project

This step is concerned with the assessment of water quantity and quality impacts of the proposed project/action in the area of its location and around that. Water impacts in construction and operation phases of the project may be quite different. All such impacts are to be identified keeping in mind the technical aspect of the project and its potential for water pollution.

'Impact prediction' as we know, implies quantification or qualitative description of future events, say water quantity and quality changes associated with the proposed project. Water quality impacts of a project have three approaches: (*a*) professional judgment; (*b*) extrapolation from similar projects; and (*c*) use of mathematical modelling.

Professional judgment approach is, no doubt, very useful way of assessing the future water quality impacts and are qualitative in nature. The 'ad hoc' checklist, matrices or even network methods can be used for this purpose, but the predictive power of such techniques is low. Through professional judgment we get just a feel about the future water quality impacts of the project.

Extrapolations from similar projects regarding water quality impacts provide useful analogy but such projections would also be more or less qualitative in nature or at the most semi-quantitative. It is often difficult to compare geographical surroundings of two similar projects.

The use of mathematical models for assessing water quality impacts is quite scientific as it provides objectivity to the analysis.

We may define modeling as a process by which various hydrological interactions are identified and linked together as well as to the water quality indicators. A model is a representation of the environment. Once it is developed, calibrated and verified, it can be used to predict the environmental impacts.

There are several models developed to take care or predict different aspects of hydrology and water quality indicators. These models differ in several ways.

Some illustrative types of the models used in water quality impact prediction is given below:

1. **Mass-Balance Approach:** This is a simple and widely used mathematical model developed to determine average down-stream concentrations resulting from a point or non-point source discharges or to determine in stream flow of pollutant loading.

   The model used for this purpose is as follows:

$$C_{avg} = \frac{\sum C_i Q_i}{\sum Q_i} = \frac{\sum M_i}{\sum Q_i}$$

where,

C_{avg} = Average concentration of a constituent (i.e. pollutant) in combined discharge stream

C_i = concentration of the constituent in the ith discharge stream (mg/L)

Q_i = flow of ith discharge stream (cft/s)

M_i = $C_i Q_i$ = Mass of the constituent in the ith discharge stream

The mass balance approach as described above can also be used to estimate erosional impacts on water quality. The quantity of soil erosion per time period is divided by the stream flow in the immediate stream segment for the same time period to estimate suspended solids (or turbidity). The calculation is based on the assumption of uniform erosion, no loss of eroded material on transportation in the stream, and complete mixing in the stream.

2. **Mixing Zone Model:** A waste stream is discharged into a river stream. The concentration of a contaminant at the downstream end of discharge is given by:

$$C_r = \frac{C_w . Q_w + C_u Q_u}{Q_r}$$

where

C_r = Concentration of the contaminant in the river downstream, mg/L

C_w = Concentration of the contaminant in waste discharge, mg/L

Q_u = Up-stream river flow, cft/sec

Q_w = Waste discharge rate, cft/sec

Q_r = $Q_u + Q_w$ = river flow at downstream cft/sec.

3. **Dissolved Oxygen Models:** A classical DO model developed by Streeter and Phelps (1925) is expressed as:

$$D_t = \frac{K_l L_a}{K_2 - K_1}\left(10^{-Klt} - 10^{-K2t}\right) + D_a 10^{-K2t}$$

where,

D_t = DO deficit at any flow time t

K_1 = Coefficient of deoxygenation, per day

K_2 = Coefficient of re-aeration, per day

L_a = Ultimate BOD in stream following mixing, mg/L

D_a = DO deficit upstream of or at point of waste discharge, mg/L

K_1, K_2 and L_a are influenced by water temperature. The relations for them are:

$K_1(T) = K_1\,(20)\,(1.024)^{T-20}$

$K_2(T) = K_2\,(20)\,(1.016)^{T-20}$

$K_3(T) = K_3\,(20)\,(0.02T+0.6)$

where T = Water Temperature (°C)

K_1 (20), K_2 (20) and L_a (20) are values at 20 °C

4. **Runoff Models:** The rational method is a widely used model for runoff studies. It is given as:

$Q = CIA$

where,

Q = peak runoff, cft/sec

C = runoff coefficient

I = average rainfall intensity, inch/hour

A = drainage basin area (acres)

For a given watershed and rainfall intensity the impact of development in a watershed area can be estimated:

$Q_1 = Q_o C_1 / C_o$

where,

Q_o = runoff before development

C_o = runoff coefficient, before development

C_1 = runoff coefficient, after development

Q_1 = runoff rate after the development

5. **Erosion and Sedimentation Models:** A model which can be used to estimate erosion rates is given by the following equation which is known as the universal soil-loss equation:

$E = R.K.L.S.C.P$

where,

E = average soil loss, tons/acres: year

R = factor expressing the erosion potential of average rainfall in the area

K = soil erodability factors tons/acre: year

L = length of slope factor

S = slope factor

C = cropping management

P = erosion control practice factor

6. **Groundwater Models:** There are two levels of this kind of analysis: 'mesoscale' and 'microscale'. The word "mesoscale" simply denotes a large scale and could refer to the total ground water system or to a subset of it within the project affected area. Microscale means small scale such as the effect of a project on local soil or groundwater.

   For determining the mesoscale impacts, it is necessary to delineate the types and quantities of water pollutants and/or water quantity requirements of the proposed project and the baseline groundwater pollution sources and/or groundwater usage. At 'microscale' level, a popular technique called as "DRASTIC" has been developed for evaluating the potential for groundwater pollution in a given area based on hydrological characteristics. The seven factors are:

   D = depth to groundwater

   R = recharge rate (net)

   A = aquifer media

   S = soil media

   T = topography slope

   I = impact of the vadose zone

   C = conductivity (hydraulic) of aquifer

   The DRASTIC index of groundwater quality for a given area involves multiplying each factor weight by its point rating and summing the total.

   $$\textit{Pollution potential} = D_r D_w + R_r R_w + A_r A_w + S_r S_w + T_r T_w + I_r I_w + C_r C_w$$

   'r' subscript shows rating for the factor, 'w' subscript shows the importance weight for the factor.

   The rating scale for different factors in DRASTIC from which the values are to be taken are as follows:

Table 3.8 Rating Scales for DRASTIC

	Factor and its Characteristics	**Rating**
Depth to Groundwater	Range in feet*	
	0 to 5	10
	5 to 15	9
	15 to 30	7
	30 to 50	5
	50 to 75	3
	75 to 100	2
	100+	1
Net Recharge	Range: Inches	
	0 to 2	1
	2 to 4	3
	4 to 7	6
	7 to 10	8
	10+	9
Aquifer	Range and Type*	
	10 Massive shale	1 to 3
	2 Metamorphic/igneous	2 to 5
	5 Weathered metamorphic/igneous	3 to 5
	5 Glacial till	4 to 6
	4 Bedded Sand and Lime Stones shale sequences	5 to 9
	6 Massive Sand Stone	4 to 9
	7 Massive Lime Stone	4 to 9
	3 Sand and Gravel	6 to 9
	2 Basalt	5 to 10
	1 Karst	9 to 10
Soil Media	Thin or absent	10
	Gravel	20
	Sand	9
	Shrinking and/or Aggregated clay	7
	Sandy Loam	6
	Loam	5
	Silty Loam	4

Contd...

	Clay Loam	3
	Non-shrinking and Non-aggregated clay	1
Topography	% Slope	
	0 to 2	10
	2 to 6	9
	6 to 12	5
	12 to 18	3
	18+	1
Hydraulic Conductivity	Range, gpd/ft^2	
	1 to 100	1
	100 to 300	2
	300 to 700	4
	700 to 1000	6
	1000 to 2000	8
	2000+	10
Vadose-zone	Range and Confining Layer	
	Silt/clay	2 to 6
	Shale	2 to 5
	Lime stone	2 to 7
	Sandstone	4 to 8
	Bedded line and sand stone, shale	4 to 8
	Sand and gravel with significant amount of silt and clay	4 to 8
	Metamorphic/igneous	2 to 9
	Sand and Gravel	6 to 10
	Basalt	2 to 10
	Karstline stone	8 to 10

The importance weights for all DRASTIC factors are as follows:

Table 3.9 Importance Weights of Drastic Factors

S.No.	Factor	Importance Weights	
		Generic Model	Pesticide Model
1	Depth	5	5
2	Recharge Rate	4	4
3	Aquifer Media	3	3
4	Soil Media	2	5
5	Topography	1	3
6	Impact of Vadose Media	5	4
7	Conductivity (Hydraulic) of Aquifer	3	2

'Transport modeling approach' developed by Knox, Subatini and Canter, (1993), 'temperature models' and 'small lake models' are also very useful way of assessing groundwater quality for microscale impact prediction.

7. **Water Uses and Waste Water Flows:** Estimation of the demand for water for various uses is an important aspect of the water quality impact assessment. Water demand will have considerable impact on water supply including waste water treatment facilities and water distributing systems.

   Waste water flow and load information is of prime importance when assessing the impacts on water quality in the receiving rivers. Because of the importance of waste water as a river or ground polluter, more and more emphasis is being given on its treatment and making it suitable for human and vegetation uses and thus, a potential source of water on recycling.

Assessment of Impact Significance

This information provides us a base for comparison of the future impacts with their proper interpretation. The incremental water quality impacts (i.e. water quality with the project minus water quality without the project) can be calculated. The absolute impacts associated with the project or without the project in future can be compared with the numerical values of the standards fixed by the environmental pollution controlling agencies. If the impacts exceed the standards or threshold levels, we have to design and initiate a system of mitigation measures for them.

Professional judgment, experts' help and sometime public responses are quite helpful to assess the significance of the water quality impacts arising from a project.

Mitigation Measures and Monitoring

Mitigation measures are required to maintain water quality and its supply sustainability in relation to demand at minimum cost.

Mitigation measures may be preventive as well as remedial. Some principles on which measures should be based are:

(1) Preventing pollution at the source;

(2) Minimization of the risk of harms to human health and environment;

(3) Adaptation or use of the most advanced technical solutions;

(4) Application of critical load approach to pollution in order to protect the most vulnerable environments, and

(5) To ensure that the polluter pays for the necessary control.

At the source level, the water polluting activities of the project/action are to be controlled or regulated. Misuse of water, promotion of water conservation waste water treatment and reuse are some well known strategies for this.

Minimization of erosion during construction and operational phases of the project is to be practiced. This could be done by the use of on-site sedimentation basin and by planting rapidly growing vegetation.

Water use and quality deterioration can be minimized considerably through adoption of better operational techniques in industries. For example, tail-water techniques are available for water quality enhancement related to temperature, DO, trace materials, acid mine drainage and several miscellaneous indicators. In-take enhancement techniques are available for water quality augmentation with respect to turbidity, eutrophication, macrophytes, etc. and lock and dam enhancement techniques for dissolved oxygen. Better techniques or water quality friendly technology should be used in industries for conserving water quantity and protecting its quality from pollution.

A serious water problem with respect to its availability and quality is being seen in urban/semi-urban areas. Treatment of the waste water and its recycling is the only way to protect water pollution in urban areas. Further, even dumping of hazardous materials on ground eventually causes groundwater to be polluted by them.

Agricultural practices are causing considerable damages to water quality, both surface as well as groundwater through soil erosion, sedimentation of streams, percolation of pesticides and other chemicals in water, particularly in groundwater and standing water. 'Integrated Pest Management (IPM)' could be used to decrease the pesticide loading from agricultural areas. "IPM" is an approach which combines biological, chemical, cultural, physical and/or mechanical means, as appropriate, to protect water from unwanted insects, weeds and other pests.

Water pollution from 'point' and 'non-point' sources can be minimized through the application of "best management practices" as determined by the state pollution control agencies. We know, water quality deteriorates if managerial controls on it are weak or missing. In fact, every project must have a detailed water management component which should be evaluated regularly through the environmental auditing.

Forest cover in the river catchment areas must be increased to enhance potential water supply. In fact, forests are generic sources of water supply and its conservation in a variety of ways such as precipitation, transpiration and thus maintaining the hydrological cycles and controlling sedimentation in streams. So more and more emphasis should be given on increasing forest cover of a country/region. In the context of environmental pollution control, it is necessary to enact laws but more important is the implementation of such laws.

3.6 SOIL AND GEOLOGICAL IMPACT ASSESSMENT

3.6.1 Causes of Land Degradation

Land degradation or soil quality deterioration can be found all over the world. Some facts for this are as follows:

Table 3.10 Extent of Land Degradation

Continent	% Extent of Land Degradation		
	Slight	Moderate	Severe
Africa	60	23	17
Asia	56	28	16
Australia	38	55	07
Europe	69	25	06
North America	70	23	07
South America	73	17	10

Several factors may be cited as causes of land degradation such as soil erosion, desertification, salinisation, excessive penetration of harmful chemicals in underground water and soils, changes in soil properties due to acidification, land filling of wastes, etc.

Soil erosion is a major factor of land degradation. The top soil layer contains highly useful organic matter usually plant biomass which makes it quite fertile for sustained growth of vegetation. Removal of the top soil from the Earth's surface causes a decline in the organic contents in it affecting the growth of plants or vegetation adversely. Road construction projects, railway line construction, nuclear power plant construction, military bases, coastal areas jetties construction, surface areas water reservoir projects, etc. are responsible for degrading land surface in their respective locations through soil erosion.

Land-slides caused by inappropriate slope stability, mining and quarrying activities by cattle, etc. are actual and potential soil erosion factors.

Desert represents a vast virtually lifeless sea of sand to a thinly vegetated landform in several parts of hot and dry regions of the Earth. Hot and waste lands of the middle-east, the seas of sand at the gulf of Arabia and parts of Sahara, the high and cold deserts of Andes Mountains of South America and the frozen desert of the Antarctic are some typical examples of deserts. In India, a large part of Rajasthan is in the form of desert. Extensive land use in these fragile, semi-arid environments has initiated a process of local and regional desertification through over cultivation of poor soils, over grazing by cattle on fragile range lands, extensive fuel wood uses, deforestation and inappropriate and unscientific agricultural practices causing salinisation of alkalinisation of farm land. The world's deserts are expanding slowly in all continents degrading the land surfaces to an extent when these cannot be utilized for any other purposes. Deserts are affecting the natural hydrological cycles adversely and causing air pollution due to wind erosion of sand.

According to the UNEP, 35 percent of the world's land surface is currently under risk and about 21 million hectares of productive land is reduced to near or complete uselessness and 6 million hectares is turned into true deserts every year.

Salinisation, a combination of salination and mineralization processes is a major cause of soil fertility loss resulting in a marked reduction of food production.

Salinisation of land is caused by both, natural and anthropogenic (i.e. manmade) factors. Salinised soils are generally seen in the area where ground water table rises to the level of the soil profile, i.e. above the 'critical depth' of 2 to 3 meters. The water coming to the soil surface through capillary action evaporates due to hot climate making the soils progressively more salinised. The chemicals present in the groundwater causing salinisation of surface soil are normally sodium chloride, sulphate and nitrate. Salinisation of soil in areas like marshes, lowlands, deltas, lagoons and gulf-shores can be caused by sea tides, storms and floods. The super-cyclone in Orissa in October 1999 for example, rendered a vast track of coastal area to uselessness, for agricultural purposes at least for some years in future due to salinisation of the soils.

The anthropogenic factors causing salinisation of agricultural lands are basically related to the irrigation practices. Water for irrigation of agricultural crops is mainly drawn from the artificial sources like canals, reservoirs, tube-wells and ponds, in most of the countries which have hot and dry climate. The very construction of water storage basins and canals, and soil irrigation can cause changes in the natural salt regime. Another factor that causes salinisation of irrigated soils is the irrigation water itself. Continuous irrigation of soil with increased salt contents through artificial fertilizers accentuates the salinisation effect. India, China, U.S.A., Pakistan and Soviet countries together are the top five countries where land salinisation is quite significant. Salinisation of soils from both natural and anthropogenic sources is roughly increasing at the rate of 1 to 1.5 million hectares per year across the world, most of which is in the irrigated cropland.

Soils are also degraded due to the processes of natural and artificial acidification. Biotic cultures (animal, insects, plants) take up nutrients in various forms during their lives. When they die, decomposition of their bodies occurs causing humus. During this process of decay, acids are formed and consumed in soils. Further, natural soil acidification takes place during plant growth when plants and trees release acidifying hydrogen ions to compensate for their nutrient intake. Artificial acidification can occur as a consequence of modern agricultural and forestry practices. Immediately after harvesting a crop, a new one is planted, there is no time for soil to recover in terms of neutralizing the low pH. This process is further accelerated by using acidic fertilizers and replanting of coniferous trees on sites previously covered by deciduous trees.

Increasing amounts of sulphur dioxide and nitrogen oxide released to the air forms sulphuric acid and nitric acid. This causes acid rains which destroy plants and spoil soils due to surface acidification. Acidification of soils causes loss of essential cationic nutrients such as potassium, calcium and magnesium. Soils having greater degree of acidification are seen as a major destroyer of forests. At low pH value in soil the release rates for Cadmium and Aluminium increase considerably. The release of such heavy metals in the ground crust as well as on its surface pollutes water affecting the people and aquatic life adversely. Several human activities lead to increased level of nitrate accumulation on earth mainly through agricultural practices. Excessive concentration of nitrates in drinking water (ground or surface) may cause blood poisoning, hypertension in children, gastric cancers in adults and fetal malformation.

Land-filling of waste may be viewed as an important factor causing land degradation along with the other environmental impacts such as air pollution (smell) and water pollution. There are several landfill concepts applied at present such as secure land fills (mono-disposal sites), sanitary landfills (co-disposal sites), underground injection or storage. Pollutants are leached from all types of landfill waste dumps into ground surface and under water through percolation. Most of the pollutants are halogenated organic compounds, organo-silicon compounds, mercury and its compounds, cadmium, carcinogenic waste and persistent plastic. Contamination of ground and surface waters can lead to:

(*a*) Destruction of soil properties, i.e. its chemical and microbiological features; (*b*) Destruction of aquifers used as drinking water supplies;(*c*) Destruction of aquatic life in recipient waters; (*d*) Destruction of ground and surface water used for irrigation, and (*e*) Destruction of ground and surface water used for industrial processing. Storm and sewage water accumulation on land depressions, brick-kiln affected areas, flood plains, changes in river courses, underground fires, etc. also cause soil degradation.

3.6.2 Impact Assessment

Soil and geological impact assessment related to project activities can be carried on exactly on similar lines as for air or water pollution impact assessment. This involves: (*a*) identification of soil and geological impacts for assessment; (*b*) description of existing soil and geological resources; (*c*) procurement of relevant soil and geological standards; (*d*) prediction of soil and geological impacts; (*e*) assessment of impacts significance, and (*f*) identification and incorporation of mitigation measures. The first step is basically a desk study. It is what we call as 'scooping' focusing on a brief discussion of the proposed project, its nature including the technological considerations and site. This will be obviously done right at the design stage but more important aspect is that to find the kind of soil impacts during its construction and operational phases. Soil erosion, land filling of waste, affluent release and its chemical constituents, etc. degrade soil and ground water.

Following this stage, assessment of baseline soil conditions or environment is to be carried on. This can be done through three sub steps: desk study, field work and laboratory tests. The desk study will be basically concerned to collect the secondary information regarding the soil characteristics and geological formation at the proposed site of the project and around that. The information on such aspects as well as other dimensions of soil will normally be available from the records of the concerned government departments. In India, the soil maps developed by the Survey of India may be quite informative for finding the soil types and their properties. Apart from this, the nodal agency called Geological Survey of India provides all kinds of information about soils, rocks, etc. for most parts of the country. The Central Water and Power Commission also provides quite useful information about soils and rocks mainly looking at them from engineering point of view. Several agricultural universities and specialized government laboratories are quite helpful in providing information regarding soils in their respective regions.The desk study related to the baseline soil scenario is to be supplemented by the field survey. Soil profile varies from place to place. In order to find the chemical and physical properties of soils, soil testing exercise is to be carried on in the labs. For this, appropriate number of soil samples are to be collected from various points around the project site. The soil samples must be fairly representative of the soil structure of the place/or region.

Soil sampling is generally done by digging a large number of pits all over the site and soils are collected from each horizon of the soil profile. The depth of pits depends on the nature of the project. For agriculture and plantation, the surface soil will be more important so soil sample down to 30 cms are normally collected for the concerned projects. The selection sites for digging the pits in order to collect soil samples should be done systematically. The collected samples are sent to labs for testing or arrangements are made for their spot testing.

A black or grey-brown soil is likely to have a high humus content. A yellow, or orange or red-brown soil is an indicator of high iron in it. Similarly, a white soil may contain higher levels of silica, aluminium hydroxide, gypsum or calcium carbonate. Soil kits for making on the spot testing of soils have already been developed.

Laboratory experiments on soils are carried on for determination of their physical and chemical properties. Some important properties are: water content, presence of organic compounds and minerals, soil texture, bulk density, compaction, plasticity, shear strength, soil pH, cation exchange capacity, soil nutrient strength, presence of heavy metals, organic pollutants and so on.

The baseline soil environment, once it is assessed, is to be predicted for future. The factors causing overall soil degradation are to be predicted particularly in the project area.

The next step is to predict the soil impacts associated with the proposed project. Different types of projects will have different kinds of soil impacts. In some projects a large amount of top soil will be removed from the site while in some other types of projects such effect will be minimal. Hence, nature of the project, its technology and size will be the major factors for determining soil impacts. Three types of soil impacts due to projects are: (*a*) physical impacts like changes in topography, stability and soil erosion, etc. (*b*) chemical impacts like emissions and deposits of different types of soil degrading chemicals on the soil, and (*c*) land-use or resource changes. In the context of the EIA, we may put the potential impacts of a project in the categories as soil erosion, dis-aggregation, compaction and pollution.

Almost all projects cause soil erosion in some way or other. Dis-aggregation implies mixing up of soils when they are disturbed. In several developmental projects, particularly during their construction phases, a considerable amount of soil is shifted from one place to another. This causes physical disruption of soil structure. Another type of soil disaggregation might also be created by the project. It is known as the chemical disaggregation in which the release of toxic chemicals and their mixing with the soil causing a redistribution of elements within the soil profile. In some cases, toxic or infertile sub-surface material may be brought to the surface making it difficult or unfit for fresh vegetation. Compaction of soil during construction phases of the projects in inevitable. Compaction of soils causing plant root penetration some what more difficult and slow, as a result vegetation growth on such a soil becomes quite slow. Infiltration of water on ground with compacted soils also becomes difficult so there is increased run-off and thus, soil erosion.

Soil is polluted by several projects during their construction phases such as soil spilling from the vehicles, and storage of all kinds of building materials such as sand, gravels, cement, wood, etc. During operational phases of the projects, by-products like effluents, exhausts, oil wells, chemicals, etc. pollute soil. Depending on the types of soils, the effect will vary from place to place due to air pollution.

There are no standard mathematical models for predicting soil impacts. One has to use the simple checklist and other subjective methods to see the future of the soils scenario. The knowledge of the soil degrading factors is an important aspect of the impact prediction exercise. The detail aspects of the project construction and its operations in the future are to be examined carefully for this purpose.

Once impacts of the project on soils are assessed, their significance can be determined on the basis of soil quality standards. Such standards rarely exist in several countries. So, professional judgment will be the only way to determine the significance of the soil impacts.

3.6.3 Mitigation Measures

Efforts are to be made to minimize soil erosion. Some steps in this direction are as follows:

1. Vegetation cover is an efficient way to protect soil erosion. Removal of vegetation from the construction sites should be minimized and after construction of the projects all bare areas should be re-vegetated as early as possible.
2. Creation of gentle slope gradients and installation of suitable drainage systems to direct water away from the slopes to protect soil erosion.
3. Open large expanses of bare soil should not be created otherwise there will be wind erosion of soil from such expanses.
4. If the developmental project is located near to a water body, siltation traps should be installed to trap sediments and prevent damage to fresh water ecosystems.
5. Considerable amount of soil loss occurs due to highway construction in hilly regions and mining projects. The soil loss must be minimized by storing the soil dugged and shifting it to other areas.

6. The compaction of soil at the construction sites of projects should be minimized by using wide tyres to spread the weight of vehicles, and by use of a single or few tracks for vehicle movements. Plants may be grown over it.
7. Avoid run-off of pollutants in liquid form over the land.
8. In general, deforestation must be avoided to protect soil erosion on mesoscale basis.
9. Crop rotation and leaving the agricultural land uncultivated for some time between the successive crops are effective ways to restore natural recovery of soil fertility.
10. Excessive withdrawal of groundwater and other resources like coal should be avoided.
11. Excessive use of chemical fertilizers and pesticides in agricultural practices must be avoided in order to avoid land degradation.
12. Proper or scientific techniques must be adopted for land management in order to avoid soil degradation and loss.

REVIEW QUESTIONS

1. Enlist dimensions of environment.
2. Clearly define and describe environmental impact assessment. Differentiate between:
   (*i*) primary & secondary impacts
   (*ii*) short-term & long-term impacts
   (*iii*) positive & negative impacts
3. In detail, describe about following two methods of environmental impact assessment with hypothetical examples:
   (*i*) matrix method
   (*ii*) network method
4. Following are two methods of air quality impact assessment:
   (*i*) mass balance approach
   (*ii*) mathematical models
   Clearly describe them.
5. Write short note on noise prediction in the context of noise impact analysis.
6. Describe about following prediction methods of water impact:
   (*i*) mass balance approach
   (*ii*) mixing zone model
   (*iii*) dissolved oxygen model

(*iv*) runoff model

(*v*) erosion & sedimentation model

(*vi*) ground water model

7. What are the factors causing land degradation? Describe them.

8. Enlist mitigation measures to minimize soil erosion.

4

Environmental Resource Management

4.1 ALLOCATIVE CHARACTERISTICS OF ENVIRONMENTAL RESOURCES

Economic systems have developed over time for the purpose of allocating resources. Techniques for allocating resources have emerged like a process of natural selection, with those that work becoming incorporated into the economic system and those that fail being eventually rejected.

This process has been a major factor in the gradual improvement in living standards. Nowadays, the most highly developed nations enjoy material standards inconceivable to their forebears at the turn of the century, and still well beyond much of the rest of the world. Much of this is due, not simply to greater exploitation of the world's resources, but to more efficient systems of exchange, leading to better allocation of resources. This can be seen by considering how easily a country can collapse when its economic system fails to function, despite a super-abundance of resources. Classic example of this is the situation provided by the USA during the Great Depression of the 1930s.

A more recent example is provided by the contrasting fortunes of Japan and Russia. Japan is a country with few natural resources. On the other hand, Russia is a country with immense supplies of natural resources. Japanese now have one of the highest per capita levels of national income in the world. They also have the longest life expectancy of any nation. On the other hand, the Russians have seen their living standards plummet and life expectancy fall for the past thirty years.

So efficient systems of exchange are central to economic and social well-being. Only owning a lot of resources will not ensure prosperity. At the same time there should be a system of resource allocation available to make efficient use of these resources. We need to reconsider some of the ways in which we allocate environmental resources because of concerns about long-term sustainability of environmental resources.

Despite rapid improvements in material well-being, which are rapidly spreading across the world, the rates of economic growth which have supported these improvements since the 2nd World War have drawn attention to the demands we now place on our environmental resources. Questions have been raised about the long-term sustainability of this economic progress, whether there is a limit to material improvements, and whether our current systems of exchange can recognise any limits before we run up against the buffers. One of the first to make this point was the economist, Kenneth Boulding, who published an article in 1966 entitled "The coming spaceship earth".

Boulding argued that for the past century people had regarded environmental resources as if they operated in an open system, which he characterised as a "cowboy" economy. In such a view, resources were regarded as virtually limitless, with the supply increasing to meet growing demand simply by pushing the frontier further forward. Under this type of paradigm, success could be measured by the ability of nations to maximise their outputs of goods and services, with residuals being dumped out of the system.

In reality, Boulding pointed out, the Earth was a closed system as far as material inputs were concerned. Only energy flows were exchanged outside its confines. Under these circumstances we should regard our planet much more like a spaceship, operating within a closed system in which we could neither create or destroy matter. Within this new paradigm, Boulding went on to argue that we could not ignore our residues. As we destroyed our highly structured material resources to create economic growth, so we increased the planet's entropy levels. The appropriate measure of success for Boulding under such circumstances was not the maximisation of material outputs. It should instead be the extent to which we could minimise the inputs we required to sustain high living standards.

4.1.1 Allocative Classification of Environmental Resources

In order to understand exactly why environmental resources create problems for systems of exchange, a good place to start is by classifying environmental resources according to their allocative characteristics. Environmental resources are sorted on the basis of three sets of criteria.

Renewability

The first criterion is the question of renewability. If the rate of regeneration of any environmental resource is significant, it can be classified as renewable. Otherwise, it is classified as non-renewable.

A non-renewable environmental resource is like a finite stock. It can never be replenished. Further use of stock will always diminish the level which remains. There is no such thing as a sustainable rate of use of a non-renewable stock.

Only allocative question asked of any system of exchange with regard to such resources is the optimal rate of depletion. In principle, solution to this allocative problem is to choose a rate of depletion which allows replacement of the stock, just as it is used up with a sustainable alternative.

As we shall see, however, the way in which our current systems of exchange tackle this problem raises considerable doubts over whether we are truly providing sufficient incentives to look for sustainable alternatives to non-renewable resources.

Exhaustibility

The second criterion in any allocative classification of environmental resources is exhaustibility. We can draw a distinction between exhaustible and non-exhaustible renewable resources for resource management.

This distinction between exhaustible and non-exhaustible renewable resources has crucial implications for allocative systems. It relates to the way in which a resource is made available to us, and the way we use it.

Some renewable resources, such as wind, tidal and solar flows, are strictly "non-exhaustible". Whatever demands humans make on them, they cannot use these environmental resources up. Part of the reason for this non-exhaustible characteristic is that use of supplies of this type of resource by one group of people does not preclude other groups from benefitting from the same supply of the resource. In technical terms, these resources are "non-exclusive" in character. More fundamentally, the origin of these resource flows is extra-terrestrial. It is not under human influence or control.

So these types of renewable resource flows do not pose allocative problems. Whatever the level of human demands on them, their availability is not affected by exhaustion. There is therefore no need to be concerned about regulating access to or use of this type of resource. In economic terms, this natural resource is not scarce.

We can simply allow people to use as much as they wish, without being concerned about the long term supply implications. However, this is the only type of resource to which the "cowboy economy" of Boulding's article is still pertinent.

Our concerns about sustainable uses of environmental resources therefore focus on the remaining category. It relates to resources which are both the renewable and also exhaustible. It is with this type of environmental resource that we have the choice of selecting a rate of usage which will allow us to consume supplies for an indefinite period. We might also be interested in a rate which will result in the disappearance of the resource within the foreseeable future. This is the category of resources, in other words, in which there is a real allocative choice of whether to act in a sustainable or unsustainable fashion.

This category of environmental resources is made available to us as a flow from a renewable but exhaustible terrestrial environmental stock. The phrase "harvesting the stock" is often used to illustrate that we are making use of a yield from the stock which can be replenished. The rate at which we decide to harvest the yield of any renewable but exhaustible environmental stock will determine whether we actually exhaust it. If we take too large a harvest, then the stock is likely to diminish to the point at it may become non-viable.

The Type of Replenishment

The risk that will happen will be influenced by the final criterion in our allocative classification of environmental resources: the type of replenishment.

Some forms of environmental resources can be replenished in relatively short periods of time through physical as well as biological processes. Physical processes of replenishment are important. Examples deal with soil structures, its fertility levels, aquifers, the Earth's atmosphere, ozone layer, and the assimilative and waste processing capacities of our environmental systems. All these types of renewable but exhaustible environmental resources have a physical capacity for renewal. This distinguishes them from environmental resources in which the capacity for renewal is purely or predominantly biological. Examples are fish stocks, forests, other flora and fauna as well as their related ecosystems.

In terms of allocative problems, exhaustible resources for which physical as well as biological renewal is possible should prove more resilient to the demands placed by humans. They offer a greater margin of warning about unsustainable levels of use. Consequently, systems of resource management which are inadequate can be spotted. Furthermore, they can be improved before irretrievable damages occur.

It does not follow that these warning signs will be acted upon, even when we are dealing with this more resilient category of exhaustible environmental resource. However, if an exhaustible environmental resource only has a biological capacity for renewal, the margins of warning are likely to be less generous. Furthermore, the signs of exhaustion are likely to be far more difficult to reverse.

For this reason, the shortcomings of our systems of exchange when allocating environmental resources are likely to be felt most keenly. They create most concern, in those categories of environmental resources the sustainability of which is most vulnerable to exhaustion. Stocks of environmental resources which rely on biological processes of replenishment come under this category.

4.2 ENVIRONMENTAL ECONOMICS

4.2.1 Introduction

Economists are often charged with the difficult task of placing a value on environmental resources. The air we breathe and the water we drink are environmental resources that are required to sustain life on this planet. The environment also serves as a source of pleasure to humans in viewing the sun on the horizon, admiring the tranquil beauty of a forest-ringed lake, or driving along a scenic ocean road. Many people argue that environmental (e.g., land, air and water) and natural resources (e.g., coal, trees and fish) are, in fact, priceless. Thus, they say, it is not appropriate to consider them within the context of economic valuation. However, the world's population has proven unwilling to forgo all future economic activity to eliminate factors that cause environmental damage. Human societies are willing to give up certain environmental assets to generate other kinds of economic gains. The value placed on environmental assets is illustrated in our choices against other competing economic needs. Figure 4.1 shows an economic view of the environment.

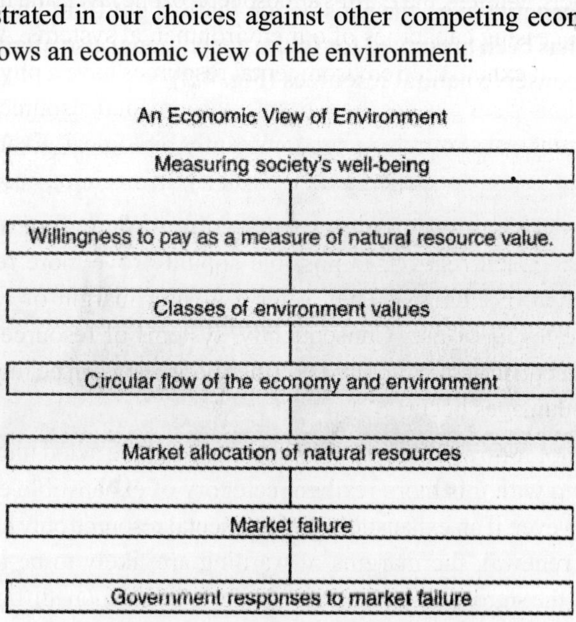

Fig. 4.1 Economic view of the environment

Economic principles suggest that the well-being of a society can be measured as the sum of all the individuals' level of well-being. This well-being, or "utility," is not derived solely from purchasing and consuming goods as well as services. However, it is also derived from things like safety, and our physical, mental, and spiritual well-being.

The fact that all these things have utility is evident, because we are willing to trade our time, effort, money, and other resources to get them. The utility or degree of satisfaction experienced by individuals, and thus society, can be quantified in terms of the "willingness to pay" for goods and services, including environmental resources. In many cases, individuals do not pay for the environmental benefits they receive. However, their willingness to pay for these benefits can be derived from surveys, observed behavior, or other methods. The willingness-to-pay concept is key in environmental valuation. It grants analyst a framework upon which individual preferences are examined and measured. Positive preferences for environmental resources translate into an expressed or observed willingness to pay for them. Conversely, individuals are not willing to pay for environmental resources that they do not value.

Coastal areas contain resource-rich environmental systems. These systems provide a broad spectrum of services to humankind. From recreational opportunities, such as hiking and wildlife observation to the harvesting of fish and other seafood for human consumption, coastal habitats provide many direct benefits. Indirect benefits (e.g., biological support and water and air purification) and non-use benefits (e.g., the satisfaction that we get from knowing that the environment has been preserved for future generations) also affect the decision to exploit or conserve natural resources (Fig. 4.2).

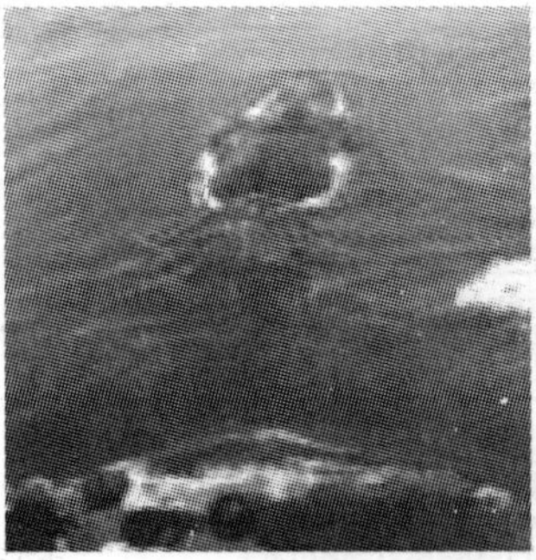

(a)

(b)

Contd...

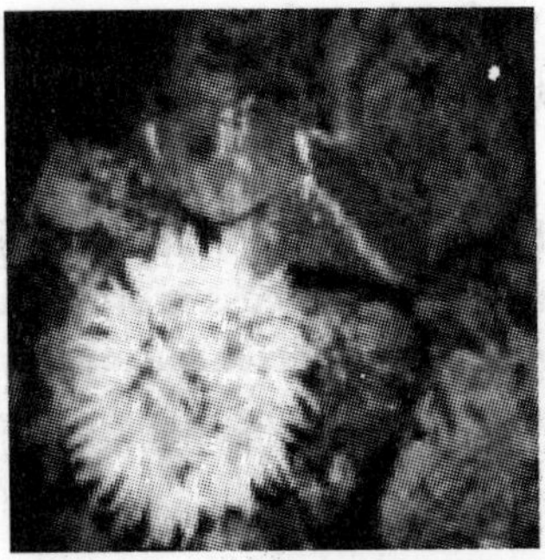

(c)

(d)

Fig. 4.2 Direct benefits of the coastal environment include (a) whale watching and (b) shrimp harvesting, while an indirect benefit is (c) the habitat provided. Non-use benefits are derived from the satisfaction of knowing an area will be preserved for future generations (d).

Natural resources are also valuable in the production of other goods. The output of any firm is a function of several important inputs. They are called "factors of production." The factors of production include labor, capital (such as buildings and machinery), and an array of environmental inputs. These environmental inputs include the land upon which production takes place, raw materials extracted from the environment, such as minerals and timber, and often, clean air and water. It is sometimes, possible to offset decline in the natural resources required in production processes by increasing labor and capital. However, environmental depletion and damage ultimately lead to declining input availability. Furthermore, it also leads to reductions of output and utility.

The decisions society makes about how to use its natural and other resources involve tradeoffs. All other things being equal, when we decide to increase the flow of one service of coastal resources for example (e.g., fish nursery), we are also implicitly deciding to decrease the flow of another service (e.g., disposal of wastewater). In other words, our decision to harvest fish is tied to a decision to damage the fisheries output by disposing of polluted wastewater.

The decisions we make regarding resource use are governed by scarcity. To economists, scarcity is a function of supply and demand. If resources are highly valued, it is because they are scarce and the demands placed upon those resources are large relative to their availability. Further, the decision of how to allocate these scarce resources has an impact on all sectors of the economy. It is primarily due to complex relationship between natural resource inputs and economic output.

4.2.2 The Circular Flow of the Economy and the Environment

The economy and the environment are inextricably linked. The environment supplies the raw materials and energy that are used to produce the goods that we consume. Waste generated by this production process is either recycled or dumped back into the environment. Figure 4.3, represents a small part of the overall picture, and partially demonstrates the interconnectivity of the economy and environment.

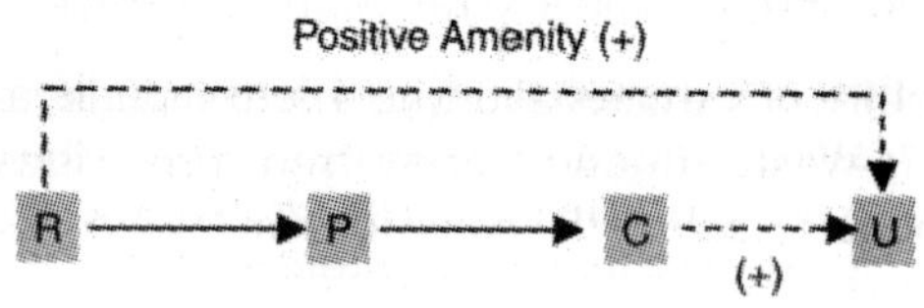

Fig. 4.3 Resource inputs and positive amenity creates utility.

The relationship between the economy and environment does not represent an open, linear process. It is rather illustrative of a closed, circular system. Within the environment and economic flow diagram (Fig. 4.3), raw materials (R) are used as inputs into the production process (P) that creates the goods consumed by households (C). The end result of production and consumption is the creation of utility (U) or satisfaction. Thus, the function of the environment, as highlighted within the diagram, is to provide material inputs into the production process and positive amenity to humankind.

In Fig. 4.4, the resource box R, is expanded to encompass two forms of natural resources: exhaustible and renewable resources. Exhaustible resources (ER), which are not renewable, include oil, coal, and minerals. Renewable resources (RR), such as water and trees, may be replenished. In the Fig. 4.4, "h" refers to the harvest of the resource and "y" to the sustainable yield. With respect to exhaustible resources, the harvest always exceeds the sustainable yield, because, these resources have no regenerative capacity. For renewable resources, the resource stock will decline if the harvest exceeds the yield. However, it may actually grow if the harvest is less than the environment's capacity for regeneration. Thus, to guarantee the continued use of a renewable resource, it must be harvested at a rate slower than the sustainable yield.

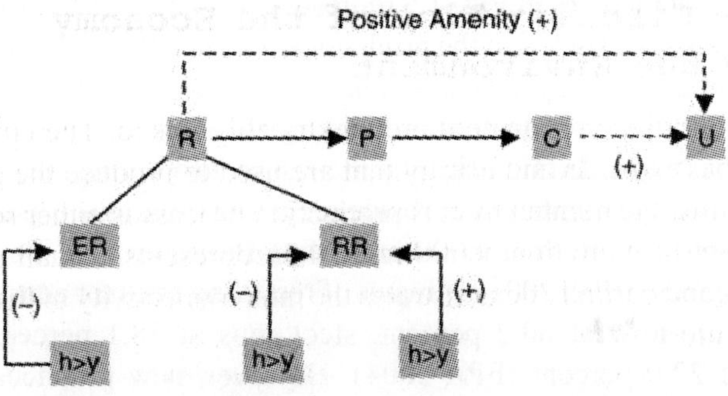

Fig. 4.4 Exhaustible and renewable resources

The Fig. 4.4 is further expanded in Fig. 4.5 to include the generation of waste products (**W**). Waste products arise from processing or mining of resources. Waste products, such as the emissions and solid waste generated by industrial facilities, are also created by the production process. Final consumers also create waste by disposing of product packaging and, ultimately, the product itself.

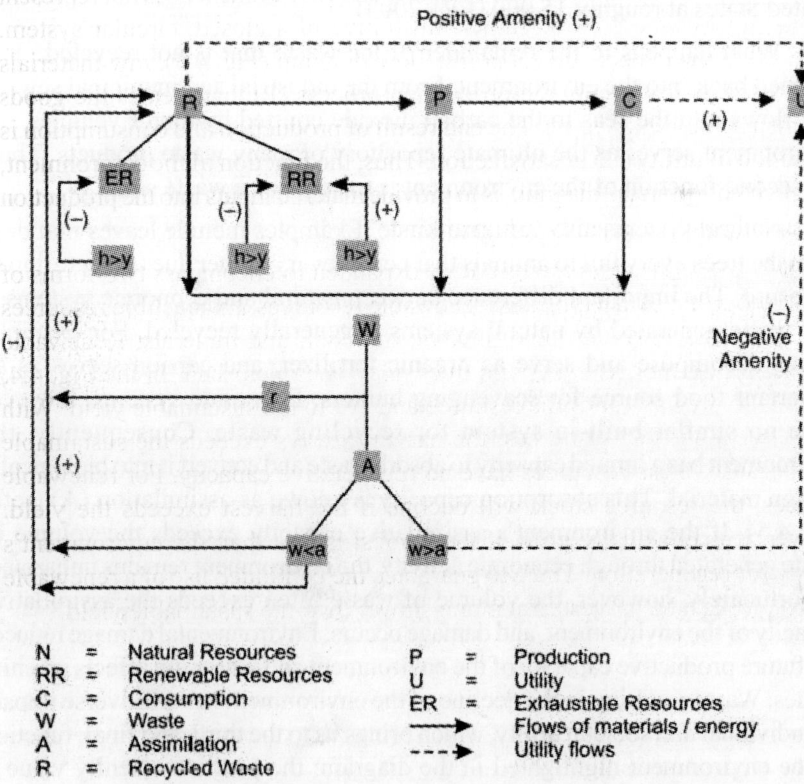

Fig. 4.5 Interconnectivity of the economy and environment

The box labeled "r" in Fig. 4.5 represents the share of total waste that is recycled and thus put back into the production process. Bottles, paper products, cans and plastics are all products commonly recycled by households. Scrap metal and water used in industrial processing are often recycled. The practice of recycling has expanded significantly in most sectors during the past 20 years. During this time, the number of curbside recycling programs expanded from a single program to more than 9,000 programs. Based on U.S. Environmental Protection Agency (EPA) 2001 estimates of recycling rates for consumer goods, newspapers are now at 60.2 percent, steel cans at 58.1 percent and glass containers at 22.0 percent (EPA 2004). However, new practices in sectors such as farming are running counter to those trends and have implications for coastal management. For example, the expansion of concentrated animal feeding operations or CAFOs (i.e., greater than 1,000 animal units confined at a single location) has decreased recycling in farming by concentrating animal waste in smaller, confined areas. Manure and wastewater from CAFOs can contribute to pollution by depositing excessive amounts of nitrogen, phosphorus, organic matter, sediment, heavy metals, hormones, and antibiotics in streams and rivers adjacent to farms. EPA estimates the number of CAFOs located across the United States at roughly 15,000 (EPA 2003).

What happens to the remainder of the waste that is not recycled? It is dumped back into the environment. From the industrial and municipal sewage that flows into the seas to the carbon dioxide emitted by motor vehicles, the environment serves as the ultimate repository of many waste products. Thus, the second function of the environment is to serve as a waste sink **(W).**

Natural systems also generate waste. Examples include leaves that drop from the trees every fall to animals that perish every winter due to starvation or exposure. The important difference between natural and economic systems is that waste generated by natural systems is generally recycled. For example, leaves decompose and serve as organic fertilizer, and carrion serves as an important food source for scavenging hunters. Economic systems, however have no similar built-in system for recycling waste. Consequently, the environment has a limited capacity to absorb waste and convert it into biologically benign material. This absorption capacity is known as assimilation **(A)** (refer Fig. 4.5). If the environment's assimilative capacity exceeds the volume of waste generated through economic activity, the environment remains unharmed. Unfortunately, however, the volume of waste often exceeds the assimilative capacity of the environment, and damage occurs. Environmental damage reduces the future productive capacity of the environment and adversely affects amenity values. Waste resulting in the decline of the environment has an adverse impact on individual and societal utility, which brings us to the third, and final, function of the environment highlighted in the diagram: the positive amenity value it provides to humankind. For example, wetland areas provide amenity values that include hiking and bird watching. Though difficult to quantify, such values matter to individuals. Thus, economists attempt to quantify those values.

4.3 MARKET ALLOCATION OF NATURAL RESOURCES

The goals of consumers and producers are in conflict. Rational consumers try to achieve the highest level of utility that is possible within the limits of their budget. On the other hand, rational producers try to maximize their profits. Lower prices enable consumers to purchase more of a good. This expands their utility. However, lower prices reduce the revenues, and thus profits accruing to producers. In a market economy, these conflicting goals are reconciled at a competitive market equilibrium price. This price balances the forces of supply and demand.

Demand is a schedule of how much of a good or service individuals will purchase during a specified period. It depends on price and other factors. The **law of demand** states that as prices increase, the quantity demanded will fall. Similarly as the prices falls, more will be demanded, all other things being equal. **Supply** is a schedule of how much of a good or service firms supply during a specified period. This will also depend on price and other factors. The **law of supply** states that as prices grow, the quantity supplied will increase. Similarly as prices fall, firms supply less to the market.

Figure 4.6 demonstrates how demand and supply work together to determine the price of a commodity. Other factors being unchanged, the **demand curve** shows the relationship between price and quantity demanded, whereas the **supply curve** shows the relationship between price and the quantity supplied. Figure 4.6 demonstrates these concepts by examining the market for farmed oysters. In Fig. 4.6, the competitive market equilibrium (point b) is reached at a price of $0.62 per pound of oysters, resulting in a supply of 500 thousand pounds. Note, however, that unlike oyster farms, most fisheries are characterized as common property resources with open access, and fisheries often become overfished economically and sometimes biologically as well. For example, the market supply curve for salmon does not represent the marginal cost of supplying salmon because of the common property aspect of the resource combined with open access to the fishers. These two institutional characteristics lead to application of additional capital and labor until economic returns are equal to average (rather than marginal) costs and the economic benefits of fishing are dissipated. When a fishery is being overfished from a biological standpoint, production will not be sustainable. Thus, any benefits associated with habitat restoration could be negated by overfishing. There are techniques, however, to resolve the problem of overfishing, including limited entry programs and individual transferable quotas (ITQs). These institutional solutions must also be considered when conducting habitat restoration.

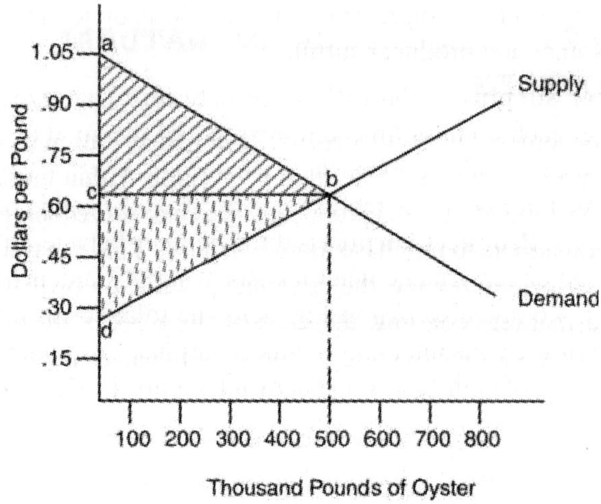

Fig. 4.6 Supply and demand for oysters

The supply curve for farmed oysters mirrors the marginal cost to the oyster farming industry of harvesting oysters (e.g., purchasing juvenile oysters, purchasing algae for feeding, growth monitoring, extraction, and transportation). Provided that the full costs to society associated with harvesting oysters (including environmental) are captured, the equilibrium point "b" highlighted in Fig. 4.6 will result in an efficient resource allocation and a maximum level of economic benefit to society. At any quantity below 500 thousand pounds of oysters, the benefits associated with increasing the yield would exceed the costs of harvesting the oysters. Alternatively, any quantity that exceeds the market equilibrium would result in costs to industries that exceed the benefits supplied to the consumer.

The supply and demand for farmed oysters, however, are not static and can shift over time. A number of variables can lead to a shift in the entire demand curve for a product. These variables include tastes and preferences, the number of buyers, income, prices of substitute goods, prices of complement goods, and expectations. Figure 4.7 demonstrates how a change in one of these shift variables can lead to an increase in demand. Imagine that a medical report hailed the health benefits of oyster consumption. The demand for oysters would increase and a new equilibrium price ($0.76) and quantity (680 thousand pounds) would be reached. A number of variables can cause a shift in supply as well, including resource prices, the number of sellers, technology changes, prices of alternative outputs, expectations, taxes, and subsidies.

Economists measure the net economic benefit in a market as the difference between what it costs to produce a good or service, on the one hand, and what consumers are willing to pay for it, on the other. In an efficiently functioning competitive market, the net economic benefit is divided between consumers and producers. The net economic benefit is, therefore, divided between what is known as consumer and producer surplus.

Consumer surplus is the difference between what each customer is willing to pay at each point in time and the price of the good or service and is represented by the area falling above the price line and below the demand curve. Consumer surplus in Fig. 4.6 is represented by area *abc* and is represented by area *gef* in Fig. 4.7. **Producer surplus** is the difference between what a supplier is paid for a good or service and what it costs to supply, and is represented by area *bcd* in Fig. 4.6 and area *deg* in Fig. 4.7. The total economic benefit of a sale is the sum of the consumer and producer surplus. Consumer and producer surplus is a function of both supply and demand. Figure 4.7 demonstrates that as demand increases as represented in the outward shift in the demand curve, consumer and producer surplus is increased.

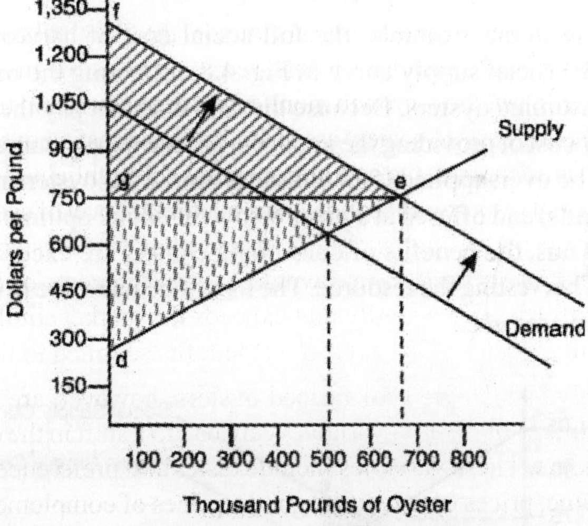

Fig. 4.7 Shifting demand for farmed oysters

4.3.1 Market Failure

The market represents a decentralized exchange mechanism that enables society to allocate resources efficiently. Markets, however, efficiently can fail to allocate environmental assets through the price mechanism if they are unable to accurately capture the full social costs of exploiting the natural resource. Thus, there are a number of factors (e.g., imperfect information, uncompensated environmental damage) that constrain the capacity of the market to achieve an accurate competitive market equilibrium. For example, the previous analysis would not measure net economic benefit if the oyster industry damaged the environment while harvesting. These are additional societal costs that are not necessarily reflected in the industry supply curve and market clearing price. When there are factors that prevent the market from achieving an efficient allocation of resources, **market failure** is evident. Externalities and non-private goods are two of the most recognized forms of market failure.

Many economic activities may provide secondary benefits or impose spillover costs to individuals and to society. These secondary effects, which are not recognized in the market transaction, are referred to as **externalities.** A **negative externality** occurs when the byproduct of an economic activity imposes a cost on society not captured in the market. For instance, motor vehicle emissions (e.g., carbon dioxide, nitrogen oxide) contribute to the warming of the troposphere through the greenhouse effect. In turn, atmospheric warming contributes to rising sea levels. Rising seas, in turn, lead to increased flooding and corresponding loss of coastal wetlands. These costs are not captured through registration fees or the price of a gallon of gasoline.

Returning to our example, the full social cost of harvesting oysters is captured by the social supply curve in Fig. 4.8, reflecting the marginal cost to society of consuming oysters. Because the firm does not pay the full economic or opportunity cost of providing the good, the private supply curve is too low and the good will be oversupplied (500 thousand pounds of oysters rather than 380 thousand pounds) and offered at a price below the social optimum ($0.62 rather than $0.75). Thus, the benefits of consuming oysters are exceeded by the full social costs of harvesting the resource. The loss of benefits due to overharvesting is illustrated in area *abc*.

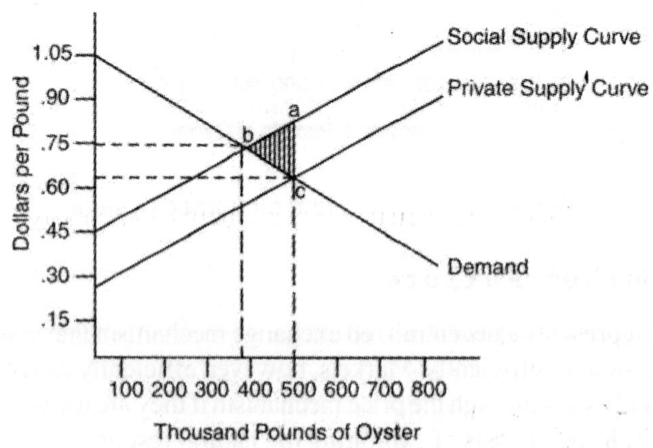

Fig. 4.8 Market failure

Non-private goods represent another form of market failure. Most goods in our economy are classified according to two criteria: excludability and rivalness. Excludability is present when ownership is clearly identified and benefits accrue only to the owner. Rivalness is present when the owner's capacity to derive utility by consuming the good or service diminishes the capacity of others to enjoy the same benefit. Table 4.1 presents a typology of goods. The four types of goods highlighted are (*a*) private goods, (*b*) common resources, (*c*) club goods, and (*d*) public goods.

How do public goods vary from private goods? **Private goods** are exchanged in a market with buyers and sellers agreeing on a price and exchanging ownership rights. Private goods are, therefore, excludable, meaning that owners are clearly identified and the stream of benefits accrue only to the owner. Private goods also demonstrate rivalness.

Table 4.1 Typology of Goods

Excludable?	Rival? Yes	Rival? No
Yes	Private Goods – Clothing – Housing – Auomobiles	Club Goods – Fire protection – Cable television – Electrical power
No	Common Resources – Fish in the ocean – Part of the environment – Congested public roads	Public Goods – Un-congested public roads – Air – Oceans

Public goods on the other hand are non-excludable and non-rival in competition. Oceans provide a good example. An ocean will not cease to exist, even if large numbers of individuals enjoy its benefits. Further, one consumer generally cannot prevent another from enjoying the recreational and amenity values an ocean provides, nor can they claim ownership of an ocean. Other examples of public goods include clean air and public roadways. In turn, externalities arise from public goods, because there are no prices attached to a good that has value. Thus, individuals receive benefits without paying for them.

Public goods are at one end of the spectrum (nonrival, nonexludable), completely private goods (rival, excludable) at the other end, and goods with varying degrees of excludability and rivalness are located in between. **Common resources** are not excludable but are rival goods because one person's use of the common resource reduces the benefits that accrue to other users. Thus, these resources are available to any consumer at no cost, but consumption of the resources diminishes their availability to other consumers. Common resources tend to be overexploited or used excessively. The government can solve the problems associated with common resources by defining property rights and by regulating private behavior (e.g., catch limits, taxes). **Club goods** are excludable but nonrival. Examples of club goods include toll roads, swimming pools, fire protection, satellite television transmission, and electrical power. Environmental regulators are using the concept of excludability to regulate and protect natural resources. The opportunity to regulate a club good occurs when the government exercises its power as a "gatekeeper" and restricts entry to companies that pay into an externality-remediation fund or adopt practices that limit externalities.

Market failure is evident in the case of many environmental resources, including those associated with coastal habitat. For example, sport fishing and wildlife viewing provide an important source of recreation and amenity to the population. When private firms damage the quality of the habitat and reduce the recreational and amenity value it provides, governments often intervene to reduce the harmful impact of the environmental externality. For example, water quality permits are issued by states to individuals and businesses that discharge pollutants into surface and ground waters. Water quality permits are issued to protect surface and ground waters by regulating sewage and wastewater discharges and stormwater runoff from industrial and construction-related activities. Discharges can occur through a number of sources, including irrigation, on-site sewage systems, dry wells, and seepage ponds. The permit, which generally varies in price based on the type of operation and anticipated discharge levels, is designed to monetize and collect compensation for the impact of an environmental externality (i.e., decline in water quality) resulting from construction and industrial activities.

4.3.2 Conclusion

The fundamental economic principles detailed in this article provide the framework for the valuation of environmental resources, a topic covered in another portion of this Web site. Valuation of environmental resources enables planners and policymakers to weigh environmental policies and strategies and select the course of action that yields the most benefits to society.

This introductory article focuses on the following main points:

- Economists measure the well-being of a society as the sum of all the individuals' well-being, or what economists call "utility."
- The level of utility or degree of satisfaction experienced by individuals, and thus society, can be quantified in terms of the "willingness to pay" for goods and services, including environmental resources. The

willingness-to-pay concept is key in environmental valuation, granting analysts a framework upon which to examine and measure individual preferences.

- Coastal areas provide a broad range of values to humankind. Environmental values are categorized as direct use (e.g., hiking, wildlife observation, inputs into the production process), indirect (e.g., biological support, water and air purification), and nonuse (bequest and existence values). Each of these values affects the decision to exploit or conserve natural resources.
- The environment and economy are inextricably linked. The environment supplies the raw materials and energy that are used to produce the goods that we consume. Waste generated by the production process is either recycled or dumped back into the environment. Thus, the relationship between the environment and the economy does not represent an open, linear process, but is rather illustrative of a closed, circular system.
- The demand for products and the supply or availability of natural resources determine the market allocation of natural resources. A number of factors (e.g., scarcity, tastes and preferences, the number of buyers, income, prices of substitute goods, prices of complement goods, expectations, resource prices, number of sellers, technology change, prices of alternative outputs, and taxes and subsidies) collectively determine the supply and demand for products, thus, dictating how best to allocate scarce natural resources efficiently.
- Markets can fail to allocate natural resources efficiently through the pricing mechanism if they are unable accurately to capture the full social costs of exploiting the natural resource. When there are factors that prevent the market from achieving an efficient allocation of resources, market failure is evident.

Economists agree that markets are generally most well-suited for efficiently allocating society's resources. Markets can fail, however, resulting in the byproduct on an economic activity, generally referred to as an externality, to impose costs on society not captured in the market. To combat environmental externalities and other forms of market failure, government agencies use various strategies (e.g., permits, restrictions to access, regulations, equipment restrictions, taxes) designed to correct these market imperfections and protect the environment. Finding an appropriate balance between the demands of the marketplace and the need to preserve natural resources enables our society both to expand the economy and preserve the environment for future generations.

4.4 ENVIRONMENTAL PARADIGMS

Extreme Ecocentrism: This is unstable economy/environment relationship. Economic growth can only be obtained by degrading the environment. However, there is danger of irreversible environment overload. **Moderate Technocentrism:** Certain types and levels of economic growth can be achieved without degrading the environment. However, unbrindled economic growth will ultimately degrade the environment in an unsustainable manner. **Extreme Technocentrism:** This is stable economy/environment relationship. Technical innovation usually prevents environmental degradation.

4.4.1 Sustainable Investment and Resource Use

Views differ about the need for policy changes to alleviate these problems. They range from the following observations:

Extreme Ecocentrism

This states that there is a need for a massive global redistribution of world markets and wealth towards the world's poor, so that they have an incentive to maintain the environments that support them (52% of the world's people produce less than US $ 425 per annum).

Moderate Ecocentrism

According to this view, there is a need for a move toward cultural and economic systems that lead to the emergence of steady-state economies where development is achieved without an expansion in the ecological scale of economic activity.

Moderate Technocentrism

This view states that there is a need for recognition of a sustainability constraint, policy reforms that uncouple environmental degradation and resource depletion from growth, and 'a leap in faith to affirm that economics and ecology are consistent and compatible disciplines in the battle for the environment'.

Extreme Technocentrism

This states that there is no real problem because technological innovation and the widespread existence of substitutes have rendered incorrect previous predictions of gloom made by Malthus in 1798 and more recently of the Club of Rome in 1972.

No one of the aforementioned paradigms is necessarily more correct than the others. All provide insights about the reality and urgency of the situation. Moreover, the pluralism of interests, differing value systems and cultural perspectives that they offer is useful. Across all these views, however, one can recognise a growing concern for the future of mankind and, except for the first ecologically-blind viewpoint, a general level of dissatisfaction with the direction of global economic development. There is mounting evidence that nature makes many contributions to the economy that are not captured by the price system. When nature is omitted from economic planning, the life support system which underpins that development is put at risk. These four views have been shown in graphical form in Fig. 4.9. Economy/environment relation as well as value basis for each is also given in Table 4.2.

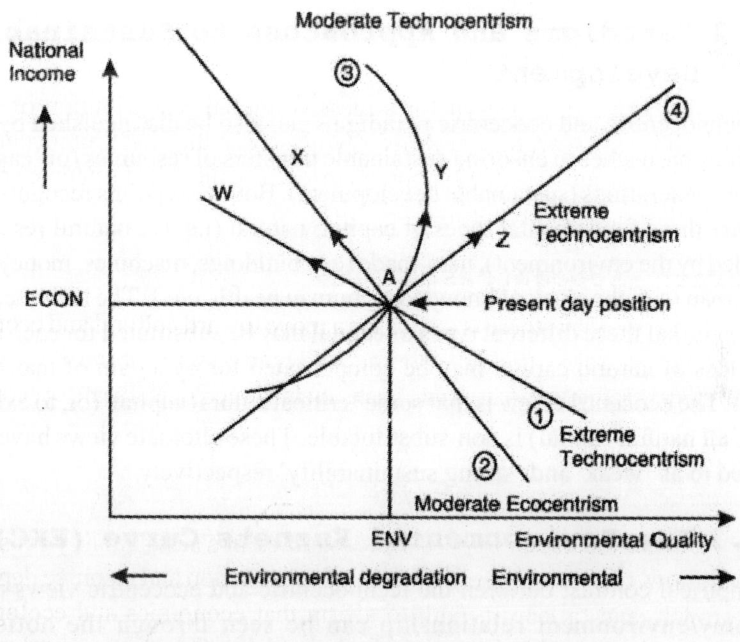

Fig. 4.9 Ecocentrism v/s Technocentrism

Table 4.2 Ecocentrism v/s Technocentrism

Paradigm	Economy/Environment Relationship	Value Basis
Technocentrist	Benign Economic growth Technological advance Environmental enhancement	Human based value arising from use (utilitarian) Individualism
Ecocentrist	Destructive Economic growth Resource depletion and pollution Environmental degradation	Non-human and human values: instrumental, existence, non-use and intrinsic values

4.4.2 Paradigms and Approaches to Sustainable Development

The technocentric and ecocentric paradigms can also be distinguished by their differing approaches to ensuring sustainable transfers of resources (or 'capital') between generations (sustainable development). Both viewpoints recognise that there are three fundamental types of capital: natural (i.e. the natural resources provided by the environment), man-made (e.g. buildings, machines, money, etc.) and human (e.g. the stock of knowledge, human health, etc.). The technocentric position is that these different types of capital may be substituted for each other, e.g. a loss of natural capital may be compensated for by a gain of man-made capital. The ecocentric view is that some 'critical natural capital' (or, to extreme views, all natural capital) is non-substitutable. These alternate views have been referred to as 'weak' and 'strong sustainability' respectively.

4.4.3 The Environmental Kuznets Curve (EKC)

An empirical contrast between the technocentric and ecocentric views of the economy/environment relationship can be seen through the notion of Environmental Kuznets Curves (EKCs) (Fig. 4.10). These map out the relationship between economic development (typically measured by income levels) and some measure of environmental quality (typically measured by the level of some pollutant). The technocentric expectation of the shape of an EKC relating income to pollution is that it should resemble an inverted U. Here at very low levels of economic development and resource use there will be low pollution. As growth initially rises there may well be an initial increase in pollution as basic consumption needs are satisfied. However, as an economy matures and reaches high income levels so the market will reflect individuals increasing desires for an improved quality of life rather than simply the satisfaction of basic consumption wants and pollution levels will falls.

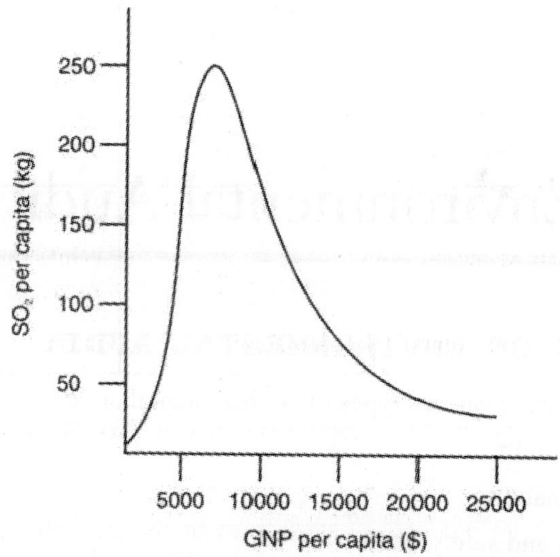

Fig. 4.10 An EKC for SO_2.

Source: adapted from Ranayotou (1993).

REVIEW QUESTIONS

1. Write a short note on sets of criteria on the basis of which environmental resources are sorted.
2. What is economic view of the environment? Explain.
3. Explain how market allocation of natural resources is made.
4. There are two most recognized forms of market failure. Describe them.
5. Briefly explain about environmental paradigms. Show them in graphical form.

5

Environmental Audit

5.1 TYPES OF ENVIRONMENTAL AUDIT

The following are the various types of environmental audits practiced:

(*i*) Waste audit

(*ii*) Energy audit

(*iii*) Health and safety audit

(*iv*) Compliance audit

(*v*) Management audit

(*vi*) Waste minimization audit

(*vii*) Liabilities definition audit

(*viii*) Property transfer audit

(*ix*) Waste management contractor audit

Waste audit, management audit and waste management contractor audit are more important. They have been described in the next three sections.

5.1.1 Waste Audit

In a waste audit, quantities and types of wastes generated from different sources are identified and the optimum methods to minimize the quantities of wastes are evolved.

5.1.2 Management Audit

A management audit, determines whether an adequate compliance management system is established, implemented and used correctly to integrate environmental compliance into everyday operating procedures.

Such audit examines cultural, management and operational elements to include internal policies, human resource training programmes, budgeting systems, planning systems, monitoring systems, reporting systems and information management systems.

A management audit detects potential systematic break downs that could manifest themselves as an environmental problem.

Management audit is a traditional audit evolved as a method to verify that a facility has instituted adequate procedures, dedicated sufficient resources, and installed the necessary systems to comply with environmental regulations or not.

It is a mere snapshot of compliance. The overall environmental objective is compliance on continuing, long-term basis. It is a function of organization, guidance, controls and communications. Each of these functions is the subject of a management audit whose purpose is not the identification of specific violations but the detection of activities likely to experience problems and their root causes.

A management audit addresses number of questions under each of several broad issues as follows:

- Clearly defined responsibilities. How are they established and communicated? How are assignments reinforced? Are any assignments overlapping, shared or conflicting?
- Adequate system of authority. How is it granted? Who grants exceptions? How are authorizations and exceptions recorded? Is there actual understanding of issues?
- Division of duties. What potential exists for conflict of interest?
- Trained and experienced personnel. What methods are used to determine who needs training? What training personnel have been given to help them understand and complete their duties?
- Documentation. What records are developed? How are they maintained? Do type and amount of documentation correspond to importance of activity? Are records reliable and accurate? How are exception reports developed?
- Internal verification. How does management review and evaluate environmental success? What is the accountability of managers for adherence to policies and procedures?
- Protective measures. What procedures and engineered controls are in place to prevent non-compliance?

5.1.3 Waste Management Contractor Audit

Some generators ship waste off site for treatment and disposal by private contractors. In general, there is several liability for management of waste, liability for remediation of problems caused by waste treatment and disposal, contractor can rest with the generator.

When remediation is required, it can cost several orders of magnitude greater than the originally contracted cost for the treatment and disposal of waste.

In addition, generators may also be financially responsible for damages to third parties derived from waste transport, treatment and disposal operations. As a result of these potential liabilities, waste generators exercise great care in selection of waste contractors. One tool to be used in the selection of contractors, as well as in the verification that selected contractor operates in prudent manner, is to audit contractor's facilities.

A waste contractor audit follows closely a facility compliance audit. Compliance issues place emphasis on document review, interviews and inspections. However, there are some key differences.

A waste contractor audit extends beyond compliance to liabilities (potential for damages to the third parties and potential for remediation for example). A waste contractor audit also analyzes the financial strength of the company, which owns the facility. A company possessing sufficient assets and insurance probably can absorb the costs of remediation without having to pass them to generators.

Another difference between compliance and waste contractor audit is the manner in which the on-site interviews and inspections are conducted. A waste contractor audit typically provides little on going feedback to facility personnel. Unlike compliance audits, improvement is not the primary objective.

The objective is to identify risks, typically on a basis comparable with other facilities. As a result, final difference between compliance and waste contractor audits is that the latter may tend to apply uniformly a detailed worksheet type of protocol in which the answers to a long checklist may possibly be scored.

The liability for the costs of remediating a contaminated property has surprised many landowners, tenants, and leading institutions as illustrated in the following real examples:

- A purchaser of land finds that the property was once used for a landfill. The purchaser must pay huge amount to clean up groundwater in the area.
- A tenant moves from a site, which they had used for 6 years for an electronics manufacturing operation. 8 years later, groundwater contamination has been discovered. The owner successfully sues the

tenant likely to have used sufficient quantity of the chemical known to have caused the contamination.

Because the value of property can be greatly diminished by the potential for having to remediate the site, the need to know the potential liabilities is crucial to both the buyer and seller of a property.

Waste minimization audits examine waste generated by a facility with the objective of identifying viable actions to reuse, recycle, or otherwise reduce the quantity and toxicity of each waste stream.

Waste minimization is the reduction of any solid, liquid or gaseous waste at its source of generation. It is a noble goal and certainly the preferred method for managing all waste. The first step to successfully achieve goal of waste minimization is at audit, consisting of planning the entire programme and fully characterizing all wastes. From there, waste minimization option are identified, evaluated, selected, implemented, monitored and communicated.

5.1.4 Liabilities Definition Audit

These are typically done for perspective buyers of real estate and for proposed mergers and acquisitions. Such audits identify environmental problems that could reduce the value of a property or expose the buyer to liability.

5.2 IMPORTANT ASPECTS OF EFFECTIVE ENVIRONMENTAL AUDITING

Based on review of many auditing programs conducted by both public and private sector, many common features have been found to be an important part of an effective auditing program.

- Explicit top management support for environmental auditing and commitment to follow-up audit findings.
- An environmental audit team separate from and independent of the persons and activities to be audited.
- Adequate team staffing and auditor training.
- Explicit audit program objectives, scope, resources and frequency.
- A process which collects, analyzes, interprets and documents information sufficient to achieve audit objectives.
- A process which includes specific procedures to promptly prepare candid, clear and appropriate written reports on audit findings, corrective actions, and appropriate written reports.
- A process which includes quality assurance procedures to ensure the accuracy and thoroughness of environmental audits.

– These features show that conducting an audit is a process rather than a mechanical application of a rigid absolute methodology.

5.3 AUDIT PROTOCOL

Use of an audit protocol ensures consistency and comprehensiveness in implementing the scope of the audit. It forms a record of the audit procedures, becomes a basis for development of the audit findings and also serves as a basis of any future critique of the audit. It is much more than a data inventory form.

5.4 AUDIT PROCEDURE

The audit procedure includes broadly the following:

(*i*) Pre-audit activities

(*ii*) Activities at site

(*iii*) Post-audit activities.

5.4.1 Pre-audit Activities

Preliminary Information

Pre-audit activities include varied prepatory works. Having chosen the industry to be audited, preliminary information on industry is to be obtained through questionnaire. The information includes:

- Industry location with surrounding land use
- Climatic conditions
- Products manufactured
- Raw materials used
- Information regarding water utilization, waste water generation, waste water disposal, gaseous emission, solid waste and hazardous waste
- Organizational set-up and policies of the company for environmental management.

Audit Team

Audit team should be carefully selected to cover different aspects of audit. The team should include employees from production, quality control/laboratory, R & D, pollution control operators, technical staff for monitoring and analysis of waste samples and an environment specialist. The number of people may vary from 4 to 8 depending on the size and complexity of facility being audited.

The team should be sufficiently detached to provide an independent view. The members should be so chosen that they would not hesitate to bring about even criticism, owing to obligations with supervisor.

Sometimes, members from headquarters of the Industry are also included. There should be well defined and systematic procedures which are known and understood by all concerned.

5.4.2 Onsite Activities

Following acceptance of site agenda, the team members visit the site. Primary visit purpose is to review documents maintained at site, to interview site employees and to inspect thoroughly all relevant operations conducted at site. It is intensive and thorough process of data collection. Onsite activities include:

- Deriving material balance
- Evaluation of waste treatment facilities
- Identifying waste flow lines
- Monitoring of characteristics
- Assessing environmental quality using field observations
- Holding discussions with management and preparing final draft report

Materials Balance

The entire manufacturing process of each product should be drawn into process flow sheet representing various unit operations as blocks. The quantities of inputs and outputs of each unit operation should be worked out for the entire process and data incorporated in process flow sheet.

A comparison of these requirements with actually used raw materials in industry gives an indication whether they are used in excess of requirements or used as per requirements.

The unit operations should be checked to find out the cause of excess usage of materials and accordingly modifications made. Norms should then be fixed for performance of each of unit operations and wastes generated from each of these operations. The production and environment staff is simply to adhere to the norms. Environment manager thus can have control over production as well as waste generation.

Evaluation of Waste Treatment Facilities

Performance of pretreatment and final retreatment facilities should be evaluated based on report analysis. If treated waste water, gaseous emissions and solid waste do not conform to the standards prescribed by the pollution control board, reasons for the same should be diagnosed.

From individual streams of waste water, recyclable and recoverable materials should be identified and provisions made for same. All 'avoidable' waste should be completely controlled and only 'unavoidable' allowed for treatment.

Discussions with staff, peruse of records of company and reconnaissance survey will help in arriving at these flow sheets. Using these flow sheets, data sheets incorporating raw material requirement, water consumption, waste and solid waste generation, and gaseous emissions should be worked out for each product manufactured.

Waste Flow

From water balance, sources and quantities of generation of waste water, emissions and solid waste should be identified.

Waste pre-treatment, final treatment and disposal path should be identified. Production staff should be consulted as they know about waste discharge points and unplanned waste generations (spills, leaks, washings, overflows etc.). The sources should be accordingly finalized and waste flow sheet is prepared.

Monitoring

Characteristics of wastes as generated from sources are important to understand its use for recycle, recovery or treatment.

The performance of treatment facilities is to be monitored so as to check their efficiencies and to modify or install additional equipment facility, if necessary.

Field Observations

The entire plant should be inspected thoroughly. Aspects of site layout, material handling, storage drainage system, safety aspects, negligence in operations, attitude of operators (in process and waste treatment facilities), handling (of scrap and wastes), usage of sign boards, instruction, colour codes etc. should be observed.

Attitude and technical capability of staff including senior management should be observed as it is very critical in achieving the goal of safer environment. The training requirements can be assessed based on these observations.

Draft Report

After completing previous 5 activities, a draft report should be prepared with findings and possible recommendations. Draft report should be presented before senior management and all concerned aspects should be thoroughly discussed. Following guidelines apply to audit report:

- Be clear and concise.
- Should distinguish between isolated incidents and chronic problems.
- Should state facts as discovered.
- Should not draw unsubstantiated conclusions.
- Should state nature of problem clearly and exactly.
- Should give regulatory or management practice citations (citing where requirements have not been met).

Audit is an improvement tool. Audit team should present recommendations in addition to a set of findings. Recommendations should be presented in a separate report so that they could be protected under the attorney work product privilege. The recommendations should be presented in a 'value added format', that will provide foundation for implementing corrective actions and ultimately designing an efficient, manageable facility compliance system. For each negative finding, report should provide:

- Description of specific requirements.
- Potential liabilities associated with negative findings.
- Recommended corrective action.

However, recommendations should not represent complete work plans.

5.4.3 Post-audit Activities

It can be seen that an audit program helps to troubleshoot potential violations of regulations and excursions from good management services. However, without an action plan to address the problems and its cause, the next audit may find the same shortcoming.

Therefore, after an audit plan is completed the facility must develop an action plan, a written response to the audit that specifies a clear set of actions and tasks with deadlines. It also clearly identifies the person responsible for implementing each action. A system of tracking deadlines to see that they are met should be established. Follow–through on audit findings is very important.

If a regulatory agency discovers that a facility has conducted an audit and did not attempt to resolve the findings, the agencies responsible will probably be much harsher than if the audit had never taken place.

The final report may, if necessary, be sent to the top management for comments, so as to make further modifications.

Other important features of environmental audit have been covered in remaining sections.

5.5 PROGRAM PLANNING

A compliance audit program consists of many elements, including a visit to the plant. Prior to the actual visit, it is essential to plan the overall program.

Planning would include obtaining commitment by management, defining the objectives as well as requirements and developing an information management system.

It is also important to organize audit team and make sure that program has resources as well as tools necessary to address the issues that need to be investigated.

In addition, one must consider the legal measures which may be appropriate to protect the results of the program.

Hence, the audit program must be tailored to meet the needs of the facility being audited.

5.6 COMMITMENT BY MANAGEMENT

No complete audit program can be successful without the clear commitment of senior management. This commitment must come before the start of process in two ways.

Firstly, management must provide program with necessary resources and if necessary, direct plant personnel to provide access to cooperate with auditors during the process.

Otherwise, it is critical that management articulates an explicit written commitment to follow-up an audit findings and correct problems that audit will uncover.

Undertaking an audit program without commitment to cure the ills that it may uncover is probably worse than not conducting an audit at all. Not correcting such faults suggests to employees that compliance is not a high priority item.

Further, leaving them uncorrected, with statements in a file that they were known, is viewed by regulatory agency as flagrant disregard for the environment and will likely result in severe penalties.

Finding a violation, correcting it and reporting it to the appropriate agencies is viewed by agencies as one of the strongest benefits of a compliance audit program.

5.7 DEFINITION OF REQUIREMENTS

Process of auditing begins by deciding what type of audit is needed (goal is to ensure compliance to minimize waste generation or to look for liabilities that might be there from past practices for example).

After selecting needed type of audit, auditor must define scope of audit, whether, are all areas of environmental management is to be covered or only one specific part.

A compliance audit could cover all or just part of various environmental management topics. A comprehensive compliance audit would address all topics and perhaps related health, safety as well as transportation requirements.

After selecting type of audit and its scope, other decisions need to be made. How will successful performance be measured over time? How frequently auditing is done and results reported? These all are important to evaluate prior to designing the actual audit process and type of resources as well as techniques needed to conduct actual audit.

Combination of tight schedules and difficult to define liabilities clearly reduces the certainty of finding of property transfer audit.

Decided advantage of having full knowledge of such liabilities during negotiations over selling price will compel some parties to seek a thorough audit. The level of detail to which such audit is conducted depends on characteristics and history of site and time constraints set by transaction schedule.

Underdeveloped or residential property requires lower level of scrutiny than industrial facilities. For latter, thorough audit will include following issues:

- Soil groundwater contamination.
- Presence of hazardous waste.
- Waste discharge to receiving waters.
- Proper permits and compliance.
- Presence of underground tanks.
- Special issues (asbestos, radon etc.).

5.8 CONFIDENTIALITY

It is appropriate to conduct audit under legal arrangements to protect confidentiality. It is important to plan this carefully, because, such legal protections may withstand challenge only if they are built into the auditing process.

The reasons for holding auditing confidential go beyond the direct connection of finding violations.

Audit report may describe proprietary business information for example. There may also be potential for an adverse community reaction to sensitive information if not communicated clearly in appropriate forum.

There is even potential for self incrimination if disclosed violations carry criminal penalties. Many of these concerns will disappear by developing an effective strategy for correcting problems noted by the audit. Oral reporting will eliminate concern with disclosing highly sensitive issues.

5.9 ORGANIZATION OF AUDITING PROGRAM

After defining objectives for audit programme, next step is to organize the programme.

Questions like frequency of re-audits, scheduling of audits for multiple sites has to be answered. Also, will the audit programme be conducted by environmental consultants or will it be done by corporate staff as part of their normal jobs? Third alternative is to have audit managed by small corporate oversight group with audit function being conducted by staff from operating divisions.

These groups (consultants, corporate staff and operating staff) has advantages and disadvantages in its approach to different issues. Mature, successful auditing programmes tend to integrate participation by all three groups.

5.10 TEAM OF AUDITING SPECIALISTS

Successful auditing requires team effort. It is directed by a team leader and supported by auditor specialists. This selection of team has major influence on the success of the audit. The size and makeup of team depends on the size of facility and complexity of issues that must be addressed. Auditors need to be expert in federal and state environmental regulations as well as sometimes in local regulations.

They have to know specific regulations that apply to facility's particular operations and also possess knowledge of peer facilities. For a manufacturing facility, team needs to know details of production process (how facility operates, how manufacturing processes function, where things could be hidden and how things are most likely to fail).

Auditors should have knowledge of waste treatment and pollution control technology. They need knowledge of information management systems and general management techniques. In summary, comprehensive audit team would offer specific experience in engineering regulatory analysis, regulatory enforcement chemistry, production and perhaps geology as well as community relations. An audit can function with team of just two experienced individuals, a regulatory specialist and an engineer. More complex facilities require additional team members.

Auditing team should also have both training and experience in conducting audits. The auditors should be independent (free and capable of investigating topic thoroughly and completely, probing appropriately through document reviews and interviews).

Finally, the team members should have sensitivity, with ability to communicate accurately and appropriately with different levels of personnel.

5.11 PRE-VISIT DATA COLLECTION

Auditing usually requires facility staff to complete and return a pre-visit questionnaire that familiarizes the audit team with operations of the facility, its regulatory standing and environmental setting. Entering the facility without this information will result in wasting valuable on-site time instead of evaluating specific issues.

Completed pre-visit questionnaire should be received before finalizing audit team. The responses will identify whether special expertise will be needed in the audit team as well as special equipment and materials.

Pre-visit questionnaire provides critical information necessary to plan audit and includes the following:

- A management chart showing key personnel and their line and staff responsibilities.
- A site layout showing location of various operations, particularly key items which should be examined (waste storage areas, sewer locations, drainage systems, underground storage tanks, groundwater monitoring wells etc.).
- Brief description and block diagram of operating processes and any pollution control units, showing recent and planned modifications. Block diagrams allow audit team to anticipate type of chemicals handled by the facility as well as environmental emissions and wastes generated by the process. The team can preview pertinent environmental regulations and compile data on specific chemicals, appropriate maintenance programmes and other information. This will help them to be more fully prepared for on-site audit.
- List of all major waste type generated and how each is managed.
- List of all environmental regulatory permits of site with copies. Permit information tells what type of reporting is required and what limits are in place. Lack of permits for certain activities would alert auditor to potential omissions based on knowledge of similar operations.
- All major environmental plans and policy manuals. Spill prevention and control plans provide relevant information about facility and issues related to storage of waste and hazardous materials for example. It could also include inspection programmes, structural and non-structural controls that should be in place to prevent spills.
- Information about non-compliance history. It is particularly useful, because, it allows auditor to concentrate on areas that have attracted regulatory attention and would likely receive close regulatory scrutiny in future.

Comprehensiveness of questionnaire should conform to size of facility, sophistication of facility management and support type provided by the management for auditing efforts. It should be of moderate length and directed only by key factors.

5.12 PREPARATION OF DATA SAMPLING

Environmental management results in too many records for an auditor to check them all. Auditor must sample from the whole in representative manner. The sample size and sample itself can have a statistical basis or be based on auditor's judgement. The method depends upon the objective of protocol.

If objective is to define percentage of population, which is not in compliance, the sample selection must be made in a statistically valid manner reflecting potential for bias to enter the sampling process. If the population is distributed randomly, a random number table can be used. However, if the population is stratified (facility has three separate operations for example, each of which files manifests), sampling should be stratified accordingly.

If objective is to discover any violations, the sampling may be concentrated away from subgroups expected to be in compliance. In any event, auditor should collect the sample and not depend upon the facility to do it. The sampling process and sample must be thoroughly documented.

The surrounding environment-groundwater, stream, soil surrounding as well as uses and ambient air quality should be monitored to determine impact due to industry.

With aforementioned objectives, sampling points should be identified and monitoring network established. Parameters to be analyzed should be determined from material balances of waste generated. Frequency of sampling should be fixed so as to cover hourly and daily variation and characteristics.

Generally, two types of samples can be collected:

- The grab sample.
- The composite sample.

Grab sample shows only prevailing conditions at the time of sampling and can't represent average conditions. On the other hand, grab samples are useful in determining the effects of extreme conditions of the waste during the time composite samples are being collected or when waste water flow is intermittent.

5.13 GENERAL ISSUES

Following questions have to be addressed:

- What pollution control equipment is used at plant?
- Has there been, any regulatory agency inspection in last one year at plant?

- Has there been, any citation for non-compliance in last year?
- What is average of the facility?
- How long has facility been in operation?
- What was past use of site?

5.14 HAZARDOUS MATERIALS

Following questions have to be addressed:

- What is latest hazardous materials inventory?
- What quantity of petroleum products are stored on site?
- Do underground tanks exist on site?
- Where are waste water discharge locations (point and non-point)?
- What permits are in place?
- Has there been any correspondence with local sewer agency of water board concerning compliance within last two years?

5.15 FOLLOW-UP ACTIONS

Follow-up actions should be taken to check the progress of implementation of recommendations. The Environment division of the industry should meet the other divisional heads periodically to review the progress.

5.16 TYPICAL AUDIT SCHEDULE

Day 1

9 am—10 am

Meet with host facility manager and environmental manager to make introductions and review purpose of the audit. Refine schedules for interviews, tours and special requirements. Receive overview presentation of facility operations.

10 am—11.30 am

General tour of facility to provide audit team orientation of overall facility. This is brief 'ride through' of key areas of the facility.

11.30 am—12 noon, 1 pm—5 pm

Conducting briefing for facility manager.

Day 2

8 am—5 pm

Conduct audit of fuel/oil storage and soil response compliance. Physically inspect oil storage area, tank farms and drum storage areas. Review oil spill contingency plans, spill reports, spill prevention and staff control plans.

Day 3

Conduct interviews with key staff.

Day 4

8 am—2 pm

Conduct audit with fuel oil storage and spill response compliance. Physically inspect oil storage areas, tank farms and drum storage areas. Review oil spill contingency plans, spill reports, spill prevention and control plans. Conduct interviews with key staff.

Day 5

8 am—10 am

Audit team makes an informal briefing to key staff on preliminary findings of audit.

11 am—12 noon

Conduct formal exit interview with facility manager.

The audit may take 3–10 days depending on industry. Effectiveness of audit is direct result of qualification, confidence, training and proficiency of personnel who conducts audit.

The team should understand regulatory requirements, relevant waste control technologies and their operations and process. They should have capability to examine, question, sample, analyze waste and interpret data.

The management should be provided with realistic assessment of environment performance, R & D environment management etc., so as to understand different operational mechanisms. Having fair idea on manufacturing process, reconnaissance surveys should be made to be familiar with layout of plant and process operation, and to understand possible impact on surrounding environment.

5.17 CONCLUSIONS

The environmental audit is considered for broad purpose. It provides an indication to company management of how well environmental organization systems and equipments are performing and apply the best practicable means to preserve air, water, soil, plant and animal life from adverse effects of these operations and to minimize any nuisance that may arise.

Environmental audit should not be undertaken simply to facilitate compliance with law. It should be seen as a means to accomplish much more in as much as they provide an in-depth review of process in realizing long-term strategic goals.

Industry can benefit from critical self examination of purposes and technologies. It employs to see, in which area problems might arise, particularly with regards to human health. Environmental audit is clearly of self examination.

REVIEW QUESTIONS

1. Explain about:
   (*i*) Management audit
   (*ii*) Waste management contractor audit.
2. What are on-site activities during audit procedure? Describe them.
3. What items are included in pre-visit questionnaire, which provides critical information?
4. Present a typical environmental audit schedule.

6

Natural Resources and Environmental Pollution in India

6.1 WATER RESOURCES

India receives 4000 cubic kilometers of water every year through precipitation. Yet, because most of it is concentrated in the South-West monsoon (from June to September) and falls unevenly (from as low as 100 millimeters in Western Rajasthan to as high as 9000 millimeters in Meghalaya), the availability of water varies enormously in different river basins as shown in Fig. 6.1. The availability of renewable fresh water resources per capita in India has fallen from 6000 cubic meters in 1947 to about 2300 cubic meters in 1997 as shown in Fig. 6.2. Of the country's utilizable water resources of about 1100 cubic kilometers, surface sources, e.g. rivers, account for roughly 60% and groundwater sources, e.g. wells, account for the remaining 40%.

6.1.1 Overuse and Inefficient Use of Water

At the national level, groundwater is not overexploited-only about 30% of the annual sustainable potential is utilized. However, groundwater is overexploited in some states—of the total number of groundwater blocks in the respective states, 52% in Punjab, 42% in Haryana, 19% in Rajasthan, and 14% in Tamilnadu are overexploited. In Mehasana district in Gujarat and Coimbatore district in Tamilnadu, groundwater aquifers have been permanently depleted. The number of stressed groundwater blocks from 253 in 1984–1985 to 422 in 1992–1993. In Gujarat, the 1980s, the water table in over 90% of all the observation wells monitored by the central groundwater board fell by 50 cm to as much as 950 cm.

Groundwater is also overexploited in major cities. In Ahmedabad, for instance, the water table is estimated to have fallen by 200 cm to 250 cm annually during the 1980s.

Whereas groundwater is being increasingly overexploited, surface water is being used either inadequately or inefficiently. It is estimated that 45% of irrigation water seeps through unlined field channels and another 15% is in excess of what is required. The industry uses water equally wastefully. Water use efficiency in India compares unfavorably with developed world but also in several developing countries.

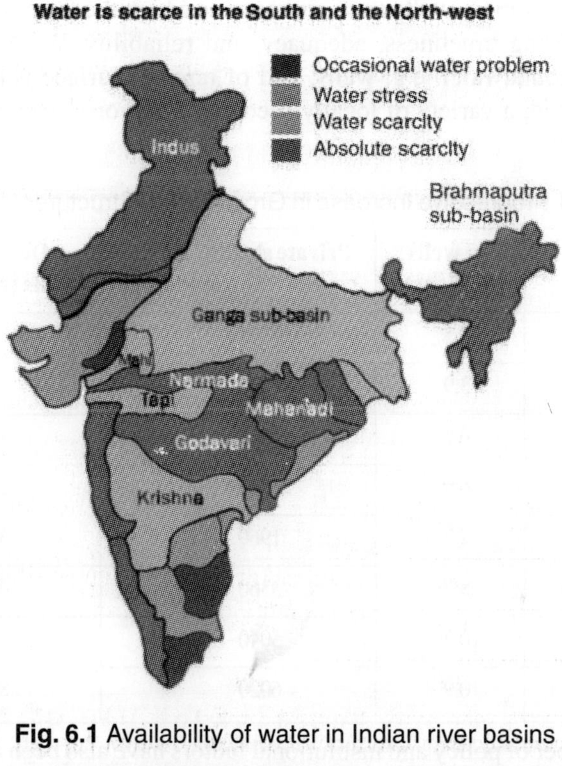

Fig. 6.1 Availability of water in Indian river basins

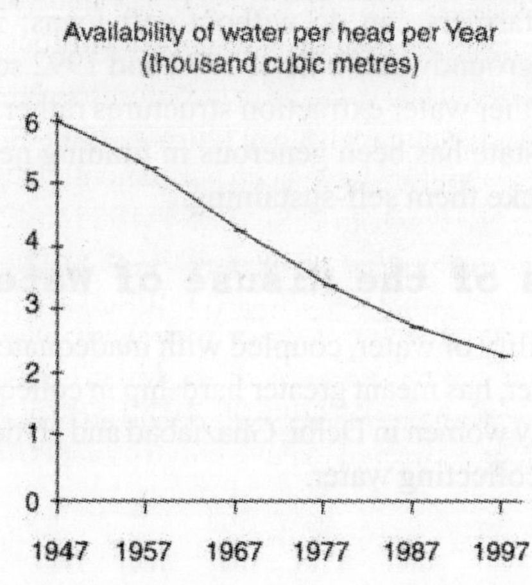

Fig. 6.2 Availability of renewable freshwater resources per capita: 1947 to 1997

6.1.2 Causes of Misuse of Water

The falling water tables can be attributed to the increase in groundwater structures; in 1947, there were more than 3.5 million wells; by 1997, there were more than three times as many as shown in Table 6.1. The green revolution has spurred a phenomenal increase in privately owned shallow tube wells, from about 1000 in 1947 to about 360,000 in 1968–1969 to 6 million in 1997. Compared to the canal irrigation, wells are a source over which the farmer has far greater control, ensuring timeliness, adequacy, and reliability. While the means of extracting groundwater, e.g. wells, and of tapping surface water, e.g. dams, have flourished, a variety of locally used and traditional means, suited to the local ecology.

Table 6.1 Progressive Increase in Groundwater Structures: 1947–1997

Year	Dug wells (millions)	Private shallow tube wells (thousands)	Deep tube wells (thousands)
1947	3.5	1	1.7
1950-51	3.9	3	2.4
1968-69	6.1	360	14.6
1973-74	6.9	1000	22.0
1978-79	7.7	1960	32.0
1984-85	8.7	3360	46.2
1993-94	10.2	5040	69.4
1997	10.9	6020	83.2

A number of policy and institutional factors have also been responsible for this state of affairs. Efforts to regulate the withdrawals of water have not been successful, because, farmers can do without soft loans; if power supply is restricted. The model groundwater bills of 1970 and 1992 sought to control the number of wells and other water extraction structures rather than the volume of water extracted. The state has been generous in funding new projects such as dams and canals to make them self-sustaining.

6.1.3 Impacts of the Misuse of Water

The declining availability of water, coupled with inadequate investments in the supply of drinking water, has meant greater hardship in collecting water. A recent study showed that many women in Delhi, Ghaziabad and Hyderabad spent almost 4 hrs a day to simply collecting water.

Overexploitation of groundwater lowers its quality by making it increasingly saline. In arid and semi-arid tracts, layers of saline water often lie below the layers of fresh water and the two are mixed as wells are dug deeper to reach the receding water table.

The states that currently overexploit groundwater the most are also India's agriculturally important states. Among the thirteen states, each with net irrigated area of over 0.3 million hectare. The overexploitation of groundwater in some areas will make its extraction increasingly expensive. The effect of such high cost is likely to be severe on small and marginal farmers.

6.1.4 Conclusions

Though we have looked at water as a resource for the entire country, water availability varies widely for region to region. Parts of Rajasthan and Gujarat, which have always been short of water, will face greater water stress as demands increase.

In some locations across the country, the water table has been falling rapidly because of overexploitation, making it increasingly expensive to draw the groundwater. Surface water is used inefficiently in agriculture and industry, and pricing it right is an obvious first step towards more rational use of water. This, along with strengthening the institutions that deal with water, will go a long way in making the most of India's water resources.

6.2 SOILS

Soil, a bridge between the inanimate and the living, is the basis of all agriculture. Of India's total geographical area of 328.7 million hectares, roughly 264 million hectares of land is available for agriculture, forestry, and related purposes. By reclaiming old fallow lands and cultivable wastelands, and using lands once covered by groves, the net sown area increased from 119 million hectares in 1950–1951 to 140 million hectares in 1970–1971, and has remained at that level since.

6.2.1 Soil Degradation

Soil degradation is the decline in the productive capacity of soil. Four major types of soil degradation are erosion, salinity, water logging, and depletion of nutrients.

The latest estimates published in 1994 by sehgal and abrol, working at the national bureau of soil and land use planning in Nagpur, put the total degraded land in India at 187.8 million hectares which is shown in above Fig. 6.3. We estimate that the total degraded area in 1947 could have been about 112 million hectares as shown in Fig. 6.4.

Erosion by water and wind is the most common cause of soil degradation in India. It accounts for 87% of the area affected by soil degradation, and the share continues to increase. About 64% of the eroded soil comes from a few severely eroded sites and soil types: the Shivaliks, the Western Ghats, and the North-eastern states, and the Ravines and the black and red soils. Of the eroded soil, nearly 30% is washed down to the sea and 10% ends up in reservoirs.

A study conducted in 1976 estimated that about 6 million hectares in 17 states was waterlogged. Waterlogging is common in West Bengal, Assam, Bihar, Odisha, Andhra Pradesh, Uttar Pradesh, Tamil Nadu, Kerala, Punjab, and Haryana. A more recent estimate, in 1994, puts the Figure at 11.6 million hectares. Saline soils are found in arid, semi-arid and sub-humid areas that receive more than 600 mm of rainfall.

Every year, about 14 million tones of such major nutrients as nitrogen, phosphorus, and potassium are lost from India's soils. Red and lateritie soils are particularly prone to this problem.

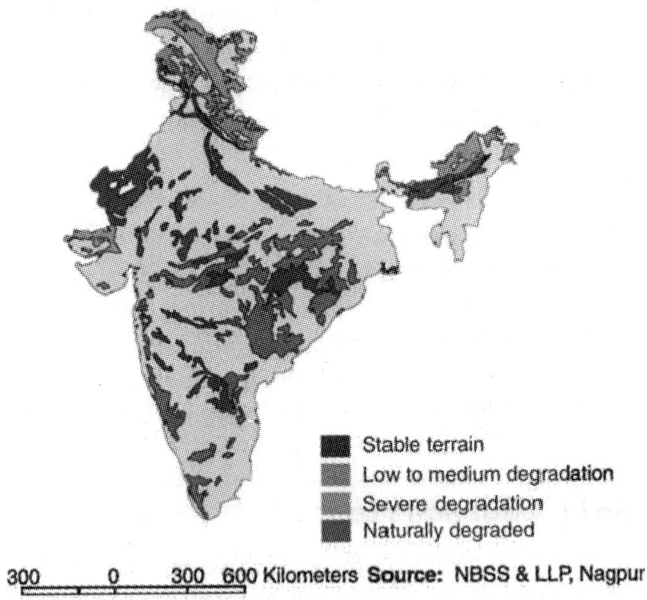

Fig. 6.3 Soil degradation in India.

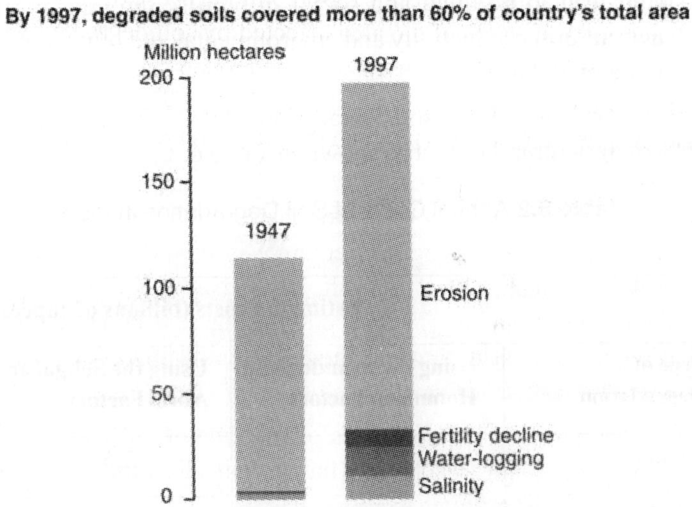

Fig. 6.4 Area affected by soil degradation: 1947–1997

6.2.2 Causes of Soil Degradation

The causes of soil degradation can be direct or indirect. Deforestation, shifting cultivation, and unsuitable farming practices are direct causes (including population growth) of soil degradation, and poverty.

Deforestation has been cited as a cause of soil degradation in 98% of the area affected by wind erosion and has also contributed to salinization. Deforestation leads to degradation when the land cleared is steep, shallow, or easily erodible, or is managed poorly after clearing.

Canal irrigation combined with poor drainage has made large tracts waterlogged and saline. Canal irrigation leads to excessive recharge of groundwater especially if the canals are unlined disturbing the hydrological equilibrium in an area. When the water table rises close to the surface it brings along with it dissolved salts leading to salinization and sodification. In several regions studies indicate that crops remove more nutrients than are added which makes the soil progressively poor due to more quantities of fertilizers, water and pesticides.

6.2.3 Impacts of Soil Degradation

Soil degradation

- Lowers the productivity of the ecosystem.
- Affect global climate by altering water and energy balances and disrupting the cycles of carbon, nitrogen, sulphur and other elements.

- Can lead to political and social instability through its impact on agricultural productivity and environmental and other adverse effect is water pollution.

The economic loss due to soil degradation is 89–232 billion rupees a loss of 11%–26% of agricultural output as shown in Table 6.2.

Table 6.2 Annual Costs of Soil Degradation in India

	Estimated costs (billions of rupees)	
Type of Degradation	**Using the Brandon and Hommann Factors**	**Using the Sehgal and Abrol Factors**
Erosion	61	216
Salinity	19	6
Waterlogging	8	6
Nutrient depletion	1	3

6.2.4 Conclusions

Soil degradation reduces crop production drastically. Erosion by water and wind and to a lesser extent, water-logging and salinity are responsible for most of this loss. Deforestation aggravates wind and water erosion and canal irrigation without adequate drainage leads to water-logging and salinity. Though each of the two problems requires different (solutions) measures to prevent the loss must be cost effective, only then will farmers put them into practice.

6.3 FORESTS

Forests are ecological systems and provide a wide array of ecological and economic surveys. They provide the poor with fuel for their hearths and the affluent a view a nature in repose. Forests are renewable source to use them sustainable; we cannot take out from forests more than what is added.

In 1995, India's officially recorded forest area was 77 million hectares. Of this, roughly half comprised dense forests, about a third comprised open forests and one thirteenth was scrub land. The composition of the India's forest area is shown in Fig 6.5.

6.3.1 Degradation of Forests

The quality of Indian forests has declined over the years. Forests are now less dense than what they are before- a decline in a volume, as it were the area under forests has not declined. Our estimate is that the current (1997) growing stock of forests which is about 4.7 billion cubic meters is approximately 90% of what it was in 1947 which is shown in Table 6.3.

Table 6.3 India's Forests: Key Variables in 1947 and 1997

Variable	Existing		Potential(1997)	
	1947	1997	High	Low
Forest area (million hectares)	63.00	77.00	77.00	77.00
Growing stock (billion cubic meters)	5.2	4.7	12.7	7.5
Annual increment (million cubic meters)	64.00	88.00	235.00	139.00

Though plantation and afforestation efforts were undertaken under the five year plans they failed to add substantially to India's forest health. The current rates at which the forests grow are far slower than the potential which is shown in the above Table 6.3. We estimate that current annual growth is only 88 million cubic meters whereas as potentially it could be as high as 139–235 million cubic meters.

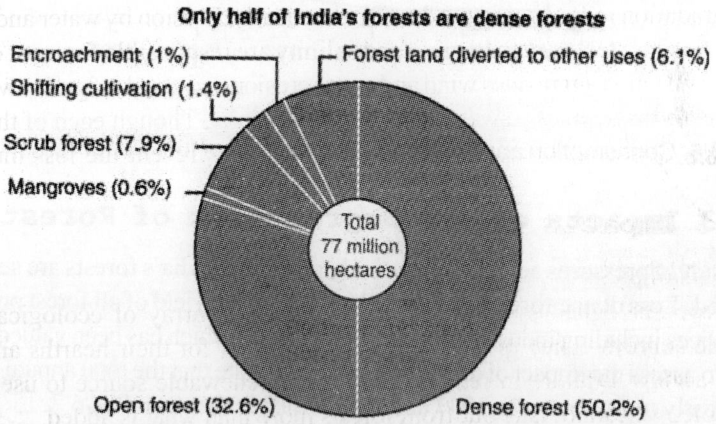

Fig. 6.5 Composition of India's forest

6.3.2 Causes of Degradation of Forests

Two major causes of the decline in forest wealth are overexploitation that is taking from forests more than what is added by way of growth and diversion that is clearing the forests and using the land for some other purpose.

Forests stocks to begin to run low when what is harvested continues to exceed natural regeneration over an extended period which is shown in Fig 6.6.

In the 50 years since independence, 5.3 million hectares of forest land is estimated to have been diverted to such other uses as agriculture, river valley projects, mining, industries, townships, roads and transmission lines. In shifting cultivation a common practice in North-eastern India forests are cleared from farming and after raising a few crops the site is abandoned and fresh site cleared.

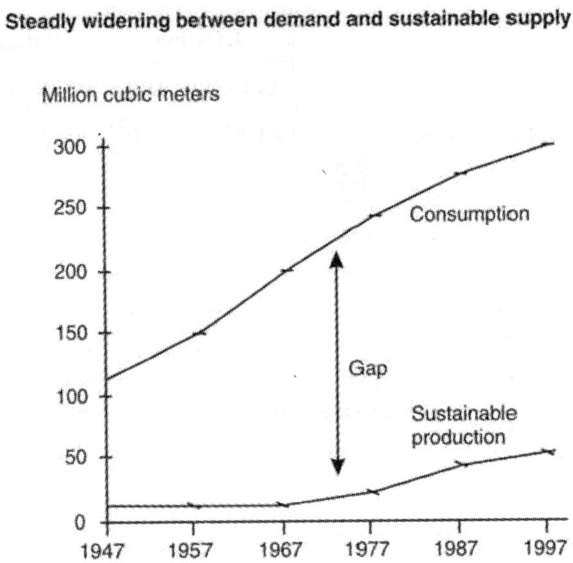

Fig. 6.6. Consumption and sustainable production of fuel wood: 1947–1997

6.3.3 Impacts of the Degradation of Forests

As a result of pressures acting cumulatively over time India's forests are severely degraded. Less dense forests mean a fall in sustainable yield of all forest products and services including industrial wood and fuel wood which has been valued in our efforts to assess the impact of degradation. We estimate that the total annual loss of wood nearly tripled between 1947 and 1997 which is shown in Fig. 6.7.

Valuing forests productivity in these terms is confined only to timber and fuel wood whereas in the Indian context biomass other than wood particularly fodder plays a significant role. Forests provide several other services vital to the well being of the environment: trees preserve soil cover, stabilize the atmosphere and maintain natural eco-systems, though these services have not been valued, because, they are too complex to permit a straightforward evaluation.

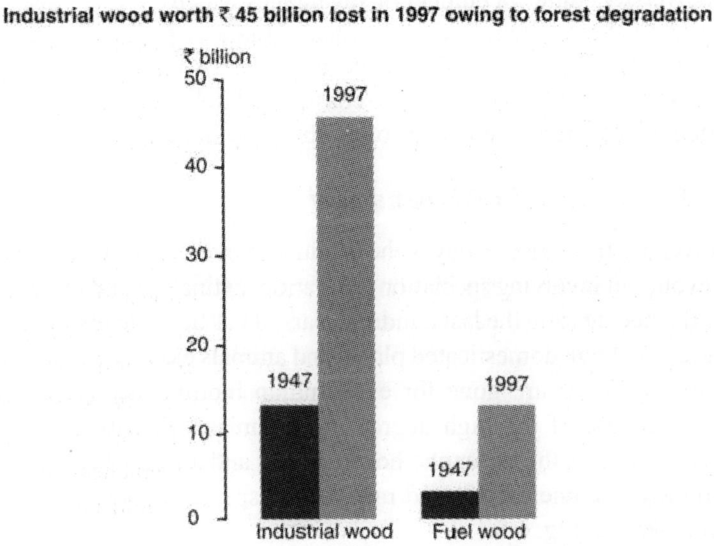

Fig. 6.7 Economic value of the industrial wood and fuel wood lost annually due to degradation: 1947–1997

6.3.4 Conclusions

India's forests have been under severe pressure since independence. The gap between the demand for wood and its sustainable supply continues to widen. Large tracks of forests have been cleared to make them suitable for farming and other uses. Since, forests are so vital to environmental health and since pressures on them are so intense. It is essential to move away from the single sector approach to resource management that has been adopted so far and develop multi-sectored approach that addresses grassroots levels concerns effectively and in an integrated manner.

6.4 BIODIVERSITY

Life exits in many forms such as plants range from grass to giant trees and animals from tiny worms and insects to elephants and whales. Biodiversity is defined as the variability among living organisms from all sources, including terrestrial, marine and other aquatic ecosystems and the ecological complexes of which they are a part. This includes diversity between species, within species and of eco-systems.

Biodiversity confers a number of advantages which are often lost sight of contribution to the resilience of eco-systems. India is a country with a rich heritage of biodiversity housed in wide diversity of habitats from tropical rainforests and from temperate forests to coastal wetlands. The Eastern Himalaya and Western Ghats are two hot spots of biodiversity in the world.

6.4.1 Loss of Biodiversity

The biodiversity that exists today is the product of over three and a half billion years of evolution involving speciation, migration, extinction and more recently human influence. During the last hundred years, it has been steadily decreasing fewer varieties of non domesticated plants and animals exist- today than before and the lost varieties are gone for ever. Indian biodiversity is particularly vulnerable because of the high degree of endemism. Twenty-three species including the cheetah, the lesser one-horned rhino, and the pink headed duck are known to have become extinct and many more species could have vanished which are shown in Fig. 6.8.

The declining number of the tiger is a case in point. The decline represents the collective decline of an eco-system in which the tiger is at the pinnacle. Its number fell from 40,000 in 1900 to fewer than 20, 000 in 1972. This brief respite of the tiger lasted until poaching for skins and bones reduced its number to 3750 in 1993.

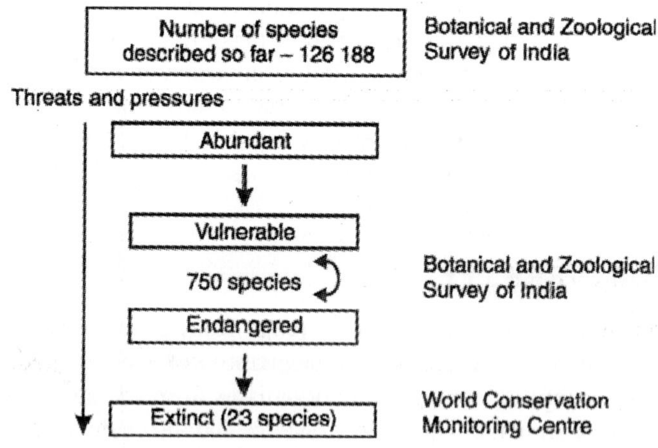

Fig. 6.8 Biodiversity loss in India

6.4.2 Causes of the Loss of Biodiversity

Three root causes of biodiversity loss are the increasing human population, increasing consumption levels and decreasing efficiency of use. This is shown in Fig. 6.9. These lead to overexploitation or manipulation of eco-systems which through a chain of events culminates in extinction of species. Specific causes vary with eco-systems. An important cause of habitat degradation in the Eastern Himalayas is jhum or shifting cultivation which is practiced in sufficient area to operate and long enough fallow periods jhum cultivation can be sustainable.

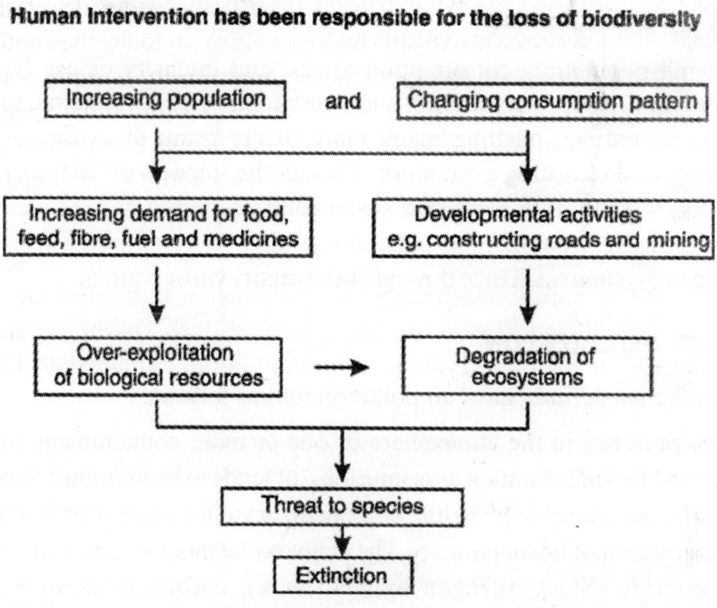

Fig. 6.9 Causes of biodiversity loss

Siltation is a natural process but human interference has intensified it to a degree where it threatens wetlands. However, population pressures have led to a shorting of the fallow cycle which has made this form of cultivation totally unsustainable. Another process affecting wetland is eutrophication. Chilka for instance is infested with the weed *potamogeton pectinatus*. Intensive fishing can reduce populations to such an extent that they are no longer able to regenerate a viable number.

6.4.3 Impacts of the Loss of Biodiversity

What we know today about the extent and significance of biodiversity loss is woefully inadequate. Biologists have warned us about the dire consequences of the extinction of species that we are currently witnessing. Is this the most pressing, most urgent, and most important question facing humanity?

Popular debates have emphasized the importance of genetic and species diversity. Every gene in a gene pool, and every species of plant and animal, is potentially useful to humankind. Diversity has an insurance value, for it widens the range of environmental conditions under which species can perform key ecological and economic functions. For instance, in the early 1970s, when rice in South-East Asia was attacked by the grassy stunt virus, a gene from a wild strain of rice (*Oryza nivara*) from Uttar Pradesh helped save the crop.

6.4.4 Conclusions

The growing population, consumption levels, and intensity of use have all contributed to the over-exploitation and manipulation of ecosystems, making many species extinct, pushing many more to the brink of extinction, and endangering or threatening even more. Though the impacts of such a loss are difficult to estimate, it is clear that sustainable economic development pre-supposes ecological stability, brought about either by containing stress or by promoting ecosystem resilience through biodiversity conservation.

6.5 AIR POLLUTION

One of the formal definitions of air pollution runs as follows:

"The presence in the atmosphere of one or more contaminants in such quantities and for such duration as is injurious, or tends to be injurious, to human health or welfare, animal or plant life, or property or would unreasonably interfere with the enjoyment of life or property. The major pollutants are particulate matter, sulphur dioxide (SO_2), nitrogen oxides (NOx), carbon monoxide (CO), hydrocarbons (HC), photochemical oxidants (e.g. ozone (O_3), metals (e.g. lead), and other gases and vapors. The Central Pollution Control Board, New Delhi, launched the National Ambient Air Quality Monitoring Programme in 1984 with 28 stations in 7 cities. So far, 290 stations have been established, spread over 92 cities and towns. Ambient air quality standards have been laid down for industrial, residential, and sensitive areas with respect to different pollutants. The standards are in the form of safe limits, which should not be exceeded, expressed as the amount of pollutant (in micrograms) in one cubic meter of air.

6.5.1 Degradation in Air Quality

Data on the degree of air pollution in 62 cities were analyzed in terms of how much of each of three major pollutants, namely particulate matter, SO_2, and NO_2, was present in the air at different sampling locations in 1994. Pollution due to particulate matter was fairly widespread and serious whereas that due to SO_2 and NO_2 was serious in only a few cities. Some highlights of the analysis are presented below.

Air in 60 of the 62 cities contained more particulate matter than what is considered safe by the WHO (World Health Organization) guidelines. In 14 cities, the levels of particulate matter were so high that they exceeded the safe limits even for industriai areas. (The prescribed safe limits for industrial areas are higher than those for residential areas.)

Air in 3 cities, namely Ghaziabad in Uttar Pradesh, Howrah in West Bengal, and Ankleshwar in Gujarat, contained more SO_2 than the prescribed safe limits for residential areas. In 25 cities, levels of SO_2 were very low.

Prescribed standards for residential areas for oxides of nitrogen were violated in 3 cities, namely Howrah in West Bengal and Alwar and Kota in Rajasthan; in 6 more, the levels were very close to the limits.

An air quality index indicates that in as many as 20 cities the air quality was dangerous and in as many as 14 cities the air quality was bad which is shown in Table 6.4.

Table 6.4 Classification of Cities According to Air Quality Index

Dangerous	Bad	Poor	Fair	Good
Howrah	Faridabad	Vapi	Patna sahib	Tuticorin
Ghaziabad	Bhillai	Haldia	Chennai	Coimbatore
Alwar	Satna	Patna	Kollayam	Daman
Ankleshwar	Ahmedabad	Chanderpur	Aurangabad	Silwasa
Jharia	Mumbai	Talcher	Ponda	Vasco
Surat	Indore	Yamuna nagar	Mysore	Kozhikode
Delhi	Nagda	Bhopal	Nashik	Guwahati
Rajkot	Jabalpur	Chandigarh	Trivendrum	
Patiala	Rourkela	Angul	Shimla	
Kolkata	Jaipur		Hyderabad	
Ludhiana	Varanasi		Nagpur	
Agra	Puducherry		Cochin	
Kanpur	Raipur			

Contd...

Lucknow	Pune			
Vadodara				
Jalandhar				
Dhanbad				
Sindri				
Kota				
Korba				

These data show only outdoor air pollution. Indoors, pollution levels are very high in rural areas and in slums. Concentrations of particulate matter in kitchens due to the burning of biomass fuels are known to be as high as 30 times the WHO guidelines.

6.5.2 Causes of the Degradation in Air Quality

Air pollution is a problem caused by both economic development and poverty. As India has developed, its cities have grown, and the growing industrial production and traffic have meant increasing pollution. Growing population, poverty, and inadequate access to clean fuels in rural areas have perpetuated the use of biomass fuels, thereby condemning more than 90% of the rural households and more than 35% of the urban households to high levels of indoor air pollution.

The major sources of air pollution are as follows:

Transport

Since independence, the total emissions from motorized transport in India increased 68-fold. The number of motorized vehicles increased from 0.2 million in 1947 to 36.3 million in 1997. Roughly, a third of the vehicles are concentrated in 23 cities. The increase in the number of vehicles in Delhi has been particularly high; today, Delhi has 8% of the total registered vehicles in India. The composition of this fleet at the all-India level has also changed dramatically: motorcycles, scooters, and similar two-wheeled vehicles accounted for only 9% of the total in 1951; by 1995, the figure was 69%. Over the same time, the share of buses fell from 11% to 1.4%. Old vehicles, 2-stroke engines, congested traffic, poor roads, and outdated automotive technologies and traffic management systems exacerbate the situation. Heavy-duty diesel-powered vehicles emit more of oxides of nitrogen and particulate matter whereas light-duty petrol-driven vehicles (including motorcycles) emit greater quantities of CO, HC, and lead.

Power Plants

The total emissions from thermal power stations increased 48-fold since independence. In 1997, thermal power stations accounted for about 70% of power generation capacity. Since, Indian coal is of poor quality (35%–40% of which is ash), it emits large quantities of particulate matter, and makes the operation of electrostatic precipitators more difficult.

Industry

The total emissions of particulate matter from iron and steel, cement, sugar, fertilizer, paper and paperboard, copper, and aluminium industries increased fifteen fold. A few industrial sub-sectors are responsible for a disproportionate share of pollution. For instance, in India, petroleum refineries, textiles, pulp and paper, and industrial chemicals produce 27% of the industrial output but contribute 87% of sulphur emissions and 70% of nitrogen emissions. Similarly, iron and steel, and non-metallic mineral products, account for about 16% of the industrial output but emit 55% of the total quantities of particulate matter.

Bio-Fuel Based Cooking

Bio-fuels such as wood, crop residues, and dung-cakes are even now the primary source of energy for the majority of people, particularly the poor. These fuels generate large quantities of particulate matter, most often indoors. Combined with poor ventilation, the impacts of air pollution due to these fuels are particularly serious.

6.5.3 Impacts of the Degradation in Air Quality

To assess the impacts of pollution, we selected particulate matter as the pollutant with which to illustrate the method of evaluation. In addition, we used the extent of exposure to the pollutant as a basis, instead of using merely the concentration of the pollutant in ambient air, thus accounting for the impacts on human health of indoor as well as outdoor air pollution. In our estimate, the nationwide impacts of exposure to indoor and outdoor air pollution are enormous. 2.5 million premature deaths in 1997. Contrary to popular opinion, air pollution is not confined to large cities. Nearly three-fourths of India's population, which is rural, bears 84% of the burden of exposure to air pollution.

Women bear the brunt of indoor air pollution; living in slums are the worst affected

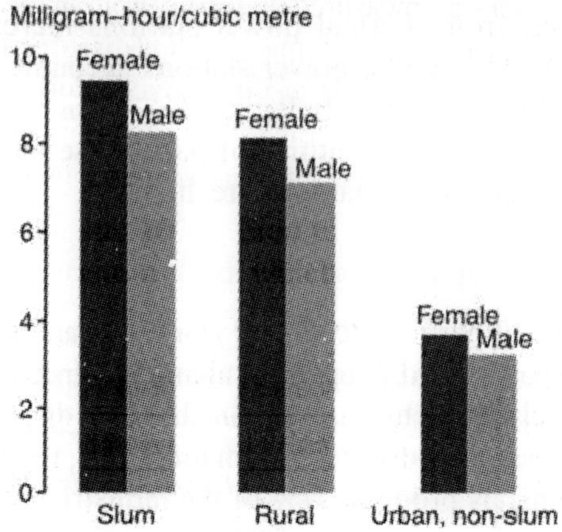

Fig. 6.10 Mean exposure to respirable particulate matter

These health impacts have been quantified for both the country as a whole and for different population groups. If the WHOs guidelines for air quality are met, the economic gains for each urban resident would range from ₹600 to ₹ 1500 a year; for each slum dweller, they could be as high as ₹ 2000 to ₹ 7400 which is shown in Fig. 6.10. Women workers who live in slums are the worst affected, because they breathe polluted air not only outdoors at the workplace, but also while cooking. Next to women are infants because they are with their mothers most of the time.

6.5.4 Conclusions

Air pollution is caused both by economic development and by poverty. Increasing traffic and industrial growth are responsible for the very high levels of outdoor pollution in cities; in as many as 20 cities, the quality of air is bad enough to fall in the Dangerous Category. However, economic development also offers people access to such cleaner cooking fuels as kerosene, thereby reducing air pollution indoors and saving women and infants from inhaling the pollutants released by burning bio-fuels. We need to tackle indoor and outdoor pollution simultaneously.

6.6 WATER POLLUTION

Amongst India's water, resources are 113 river basins, of which 14 are major, 44 are medium, and the remaining 55 are minor. The major river basins are those of Brahmaputra, Ganga, Indus, Godavari, Krishna, Mahanadi, Narmada, Cauvery, Brahmani, Tapti, Mahi, Subarnarekha, Pennar and Sabarmati.

The quality of river water is monitored at 480 stations under different programmes such as MINARS (monitoring of Indian National Aquatic Resources), GEMS (Global Environmental Monitoring Systems), and GAP

(Ganga Action Plan). A number of physical, chemical, and biological (including bacteriological) parameters are measured under the programme, but the important ones are BOD (biochemical oxygen demand), DO (dissolved oxygen), and TC (total coliform count). Heavy metals are not covered under the programme. The quality of water is described by the end-use. Bathing, drinking, etc. For which the water is considered suitable. The categories of water quality, and the respective end-uses, are as follows.

Class A: fit for drinking without conventional treatment but after disinfections

Class B: fit for bathing, swimming, and recreation

Class C: fit for drinking after conventional treatment

Class D: fit for propagation of wildlife, fisheries, etc.

Class E: fit only for irrigation, industrial cooling, and controlled waste disposal.

6.6.1 Degradation in Water Quality

Water in most stretches of Indian rivers is of Class C quality, which is shown in Fig. 6.11 and in some, of Class D quality.

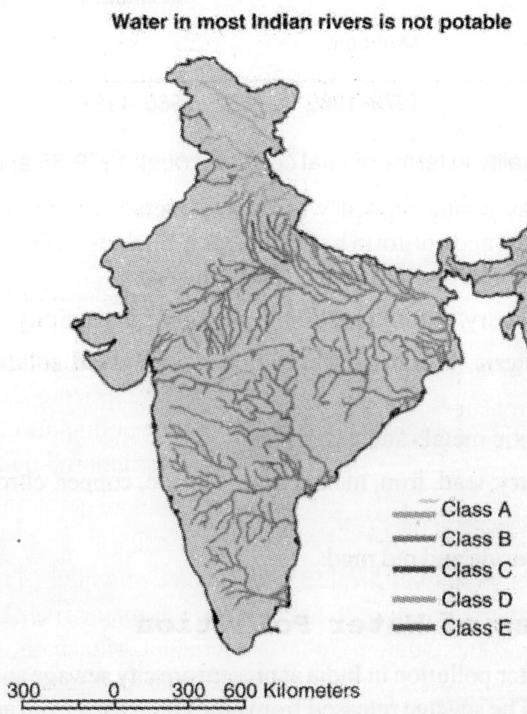

Fig. 6.11 Water quality status of major river systems in India

Average values of one indicator of water pollution, the total coliform count, rose steeply between 1979 and 1991, and the standards were violated more frequently as shown in Fig. 3.12. Although the mean value of BOD, another indicator of water pollution, remained more or less constant, more stations recorded a BOD value higher than the maximum permissible limit in 1991 than in 1980.

Rapidly increasing coliform count indicates contamination of water with sewage

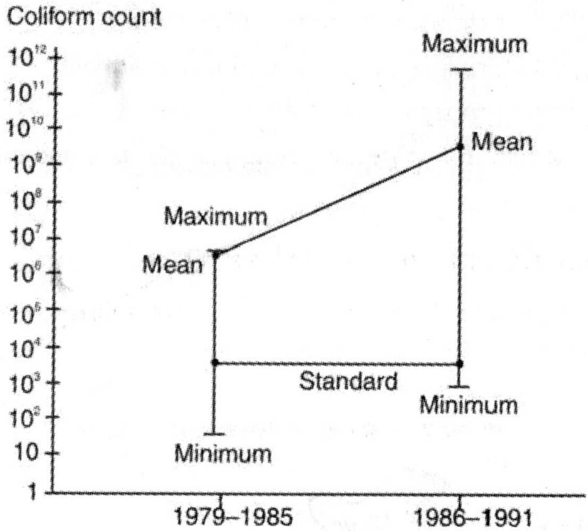

Fig. 6.12 Water quality in terms of total coliform count: 1979-85 and 1986-91

The water was contaminated with heavy metals, some chemicals as fluorides and phenols, and coliform bacteria. A few pockets within these zones were even worse, as can be seen in the following list.

Dhanbad: mercury, chromium, iron, manganese, and acidity

Howrah: bacteria, a high concentration of dissolved solids, and such pesticides as DDT

Durgapur: toxic metals and pesticides

Korba: mercury, lead, iron, nickel, zinc, arsenic, copper, chromium, and manganese

Singrauli: fluoride and red mud.

6.6.2 Sources of Water Pollution

Major sources of water pollution in India at present are city sewage and discharge of industrial waste. The sewage released from cities increased from an estimated 5 billion liters a day in 1947 to around 30 billion liters a day in 1997. Facilities to treat sewage are woefully inadequate. Only 10% of sewage is treated. Where such facilities do exist, they function poorly, and are often in a state of disrepair, because of inappropriate design, poor maintenance, and inadequate management.

Water pollution due to industrial wastes is concentrated among a few sub-sectors. The chemicals industry contributes about 40%–45% of the total pollution load from the industrial sector. If pollution due to organic matter alone is considered, about 40% of the load comes from food industries. Agro-based industries, refineries, petrochemicals, fertilizers, and chemicals are the industries that need large quantities of water. In 1947, the estimated demand from these industries was about 100 million liters a day; by 1997, it had grown to 4 billion liters. And the amount of wastewater generated by these industries likewise grew from 70 million liters to 3 billion liters.

The processes and methods in use in small-scale units often generate greater amounts of pollutants for every unit of output. Though small-scale units were in operation even before independence, their number increased rapidly after the 1970s. In 1971, 0.24 million small-scale units were registered; in 1993, the figure was 1.78 million. Small-scale industries are found in large clusters in a few states, depending on the traditional crafts and culture of the area. States with over 1,00,000 registered small-scale industries are Andhra Pradesh, Gujarat, Madhya Pradesh, Punjab, Tamil Nadu, Uttar Pradesh, and West Bengal. Although most clusters of small-scale industries have opted for common effluent treatment plants to control water pollution, most of these plants do not function.

6.6.3 Impacts of Water Pollution

Murray and Lopez estimate that about 9% of the deaths in India and 9.5% of the total DALYs (disability-adjusted life-years) in 1990 were attributable to poor water supply and sanitation and inadequate personal and domestic hygiene. According to the World Bank, these health impacts, in economic terms, represent a loss of ₹ 107 billion to ₹ 290 billion. Increasing water pollution, contributed by such factors as sewage and industrial wastewater, requires greater investments in ensuring drinking water security. We estimate that the incremental annual cost of ensuring safe drinking water and adequate sanitation facilities to all is ₹ 122 billion, apportioned as follows: providing adequate sanitation, 60%; providing piped drinking water, 15%; and sewage and effluent treatment, 25%.

6.6.4 Conclusions

Several Indian rivers and lakes are little better than open drains. Groundwater aquifers in isolated pockets have now been contaminated with pollutants. The major sources of water pollution in India are city sewage, the bulk of which is released untreated; industrial waste; and, increasingly, wastewater from agriculture. Considerable investments will be required to reduce the substantial impacts of water pollution on health.

6.7 SOLID WASTE

Solid wastes are those material by-products of a society that are discarded as useless or unwanted. Broadly, defined, solid wastes include the heterogeneous mass of throwaways from households as well as the more homogeneous accumulations of agricultural, industrial and mining wastes. Only two categories of solid waste are considered here, namely urban municipal solid waste and industrial waste. Municipal solid wastes are collected and disposed of by municipal corporations and industrial solid wastes are disposed of by the respective industries. Waste is classified as hazardous waste and non-hazardous waste, and non-hazardous waste, in turn, is divided into biodegradable waste and non-biodegradable waste.

6.7.1 Quantity and Composition of Solid Waste

Municipal solid wastes are a heterogeneous mixture of paper, plastic, cloth, metal, glass, organic matter, etc. generated from households, commercial establishments, and markets, which is shown in Fig. 6.13. With increasing urbanization and changing lifestyles and tastes, the amount of municipal solid waste has been increasing rapidly and its composition too has been changing. In 1947, cities and towns in India generated an estimated 6 million tonnes of solid waste; in 1997, the figure was 48 million tonnes.

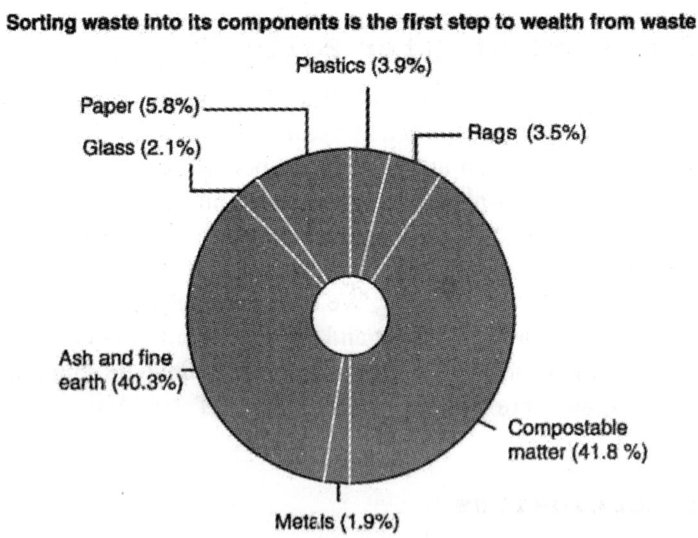

Fig. 6.13 Components of urban municipal solid waste: 1995

However, wastes from hospitals and nursing homes are required to be collected and treated separately, in most cities and towns such wastes continue to form a part of municipal solid waste. Hospital waste includes infectious items, e.g. amputated body parts, body fluids, cultures of pathogens, excreta from patients suffering from highly contagious diseases, etc. It also includes scalpels, needles, bandages, and other wastes from operating theatres and laboratories. Of the total waste produced in hospitals, 47.2% is contaminated with pathogens, making it a hazardous biomedical waste. Currently (1997), hospitals are estimated to generate nearly 1.5 million tonnes of waste every year.

Industries generate huge amounts of waste. 100 million tonnes of solid waste and 2 million tonnes of hazardous waste a year, which is shown in Table 6.5.

Table 6.5 Generation of Solid Waste in Select Industries in 1997

Solid wastes	Quantity (millions tones a year)
Fly ash	45.00
Slag	8.5
Phosphogypsum	5.0
Lime sludge	4.0
Red mud	3.5

Hazardous wastes are those that are toxic to plants and animals or flammable, corrosive, explosive, or highly reactive chemically. Examples of such hazardous waste are cyanide waste, asbestos, and acidic or alkaline slurry. Metal, chemical, drugs and pharmaceuticals, leather, pulp and paper, electroplating, refining, pesticide, dye, and rubber goods industries are among the major generators of hazardous waste.

6.7.2 Causes of the build–up of solid waste

Many factors influence the quantity and composition of solid waste. These include lifestyle, culture, food habits, climate, and commercial and industrial activity. Not only do more people now live in cities but each of them also generates more waste: between 1947 and 1997, not only did India's urban population increase nearly five fold but the waste generated per capita also increased by more than 50%, from 295 grams a day in 1947 to 490 grams a day in 1997 which is shown in Fig. 6.14. Also the wastes are harder to dispose of the average Indian urban household uses more plastic goods than before and plastic goods are becoming more popular in the countryside too.

The collection, transport, and disposal of solid waste is unscientific and disorganized. More than one-fourth of the municipal solid waste is not collected at all; 70% of Indian cities lack adequate capacity to transport it; and sanitary landfills to dispose of the waste are neither well equipped nor managed efficiently.

Liquid carrying toxic waste often seeps from landfills and contaminates water and soil. Decaying organic matter in landfills often produce methane, a useful source of energy, but it is underutilized. Thus, landfills not only fail to generate resources but tie up valuable land. In 1997, landfills occupied more than 200 square kilometers.

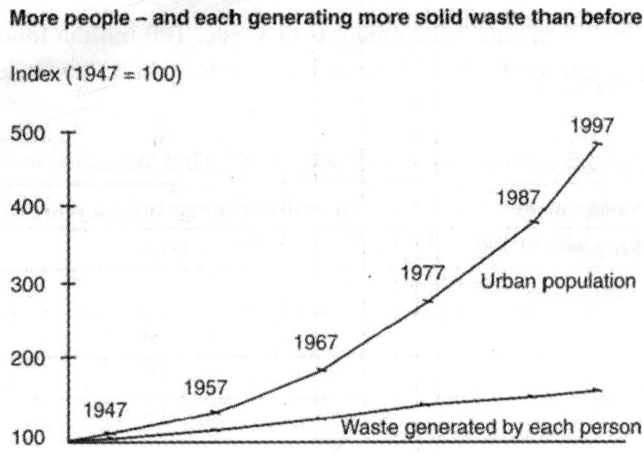

Fig. 6.14 Indices of urban population and per capita solid waste generation: 1947–1997

6.7.3 Impacts of the Build up of Solid Waste

There is unequivocal evidence that poor waste management is associated with increased incidence of diseases and disorders ranging from epidemics of vector-borne diseases to adverse effects of contaminated groundwater in all sections of the population. The health hazards can be categorized as follows.

1. Direct contact with waste in the case of workers involved in waste disposal.
2. Direct contact with waste in the case of rag pickers who separate recyclable material from the waste.
3. Indirect effects because of contamination of soil, air, and water because of poor management of landfill sites.

The handlers of solid waste, Municipal workers and rag pickers, suffer the most. In a study conducted by the National Environmental Engineering Research Institute in Nagpur, it was found that the incidence of jaundice among those who handle waste was seven times that found in the general population. The incidence of respiratory diseases was twice as high. Rag pickers are another vulnerable group. It has been estimated that some 35,000 children in Bangalore and 80,000 children in Delhi work as rag pickers.

6.7.4 Conclusions

With increasing urbanization and changing lifestyles, more and more solid waste is being generated in Indian cities but by recycling what can be recycled, converting what can be converted into useful forms (e.g. landfill gas into a source of fuel), and efficiently disposing of the rest, we can prevent adverse impacts and generate wealth.

6.8 SUMMARY

The economy draws resources from and emits pollutants into the environment, and we can neglect the deterioration of the environment only at our peril. Poor-quality drinking water and indoor air pollution are two important causes of sickness and death in India. Forest degradation leads to substantial losses of fuel wood and industrial wood and also has such adverse, though indirect, effects as loss of top soil. Soil degradation substantially lowers crop production .

One of the ways of assessing the interactions between the economy and the environment is to estimate what we can hope to gain in economic terms from environmental management and how much it will cost us.

References

- Aller, L., et al. (1987). "DRASTIC: A Standardized System for Evaluating Groundwater Pollution Potential using Hydrological Settings". EPA 600/2.87.035, U.S. Environmental Protection Agency, Ada, Okla, May.
- Ball, D.F., 1986, Site and Soils', in *Methods in Plant Ecology*, 2nd Ed., P.D. Moore and S.B. Chapman (eds.), pp. 215-84, Oxford: Blackwell Scientific.
- Barthwal, R.R., (2002) "*Environmental Impact Assessment*", New Age International (P) Limited, Publishers.
- Bisset, R., (1980), "*Methods of Environmental Impact Analysis: Recent Trends and Future Prospects*", Journal of Environmental Management, Vol.11, pp. 27-43.
- Canter, L.W. (1996), "*Environmental Impact Assessment*", N.Y. McGraw-Hill Inc., 2nd Ed.
- Department of Environment (DOE), 1990, *Integrated Pollution Control: A Practical Guide*, London: HMSO.
- Haug, P.T. Burwell, R.W., Stein, A., and Bandurski B.L., (1984), "*Determining the Significance of Environmental Issues Under the National Environmental Policy Act*", Journal of Environmental Management, Vol.18, No.1, pp. 15-24.
- Knox, R.C., Sabatini, D.A., and Canter, L.W., (1993), *Sub-surface Tansport and Fate Processes*, Lewis Publishers, Boca Ratan, Fla.
- Kormondy, E.J., (1991), "*Concepts of Ecology*", Prentice Hall of India, Pvt. Ltd.
- Lee, N. and Walsh, F., (1992), "*Strategic Environmental Assessment: An Overview*" Project Appraisal, Vol. 7, no. 3, pp. 126–136.

- Leopold, L.B., et al. (1971), "*A Procedure for Evaluating Environmental Impact*", Circular 645, US Geological Survey, Washington, D.C.
- Munn, R.E., (1979), "*Environmental Impact Assessment: Principles and Procedures, Series*" SCOPE 5, 2nd Ed. John Wiley and Sons.
- Peter Morris Jeremy Biggs, (1996), Water; Ch. 10, in Peter Morris and Rikki Terivel (Ed.) *"Methods of Environmental Impact Assessment"* U.C.L. Press.
- Rao, M.N. and Dutta, A.K., (2007), "*Waste Water Treatment*", Oxford & IBH Publishing Co. Pvt. Ltd.
- Rau, J.G. and D.C. Wooten (1985), "*Environment Impact Analysis Handbook*", N.Y. McGraw-Hill Inc.
- Singh, S.K., (1993), "*Environmental Conservation*", Educational Development Division, BITS Pilani.
- TERI, State of Environment Report, India.
- U.S. Economic Development Administration (1973), "*Final Environmental Statement*", Fruit/Church Industrial Park, Fresno, California, Washington.
- Warner, M.L., (1973), "*Environmental Impact Analysis: An Examination of Three Methodologies*", Ph. D. Dissertation, University of Wisconsin, Madison.
- Westman, W.E. (1985), "*Ecology Impact Assessment and Environmental Planning*", (pp. 10–14) John Wiley and Sons, New York.

Internet References

http://images.botany.org

http://ths.sps.lane.edu

http://www.csc.noaa.gov

http://www.noaa.gov

http://www.sinauer.com

http://www.uea.ac.uk/menu/acad_depts/env/all teaching/envecon/

